Glitter and Glue

101 creative craft ideas
for use with under-fives

Annette Oliver

Scripture Union

To Glyn
Who believes in me, and inspires me –
Thank you

Scripture Union, 207–209 Queensway, Bletchley, MK2 2EB, England.
www.scriptureunion.org.uk

Scripture Union is an international Christian charity working with churches in more than 130 countries providing resources to bring the good news about Jesus Christ to children, young people and families – and to encourage them to develop spiritually through the Bible and prayer.

As well as a network of volunteers, staff and associates who run holidays, church-based events and school Christian groups, Scripture Union produces a wide range of publications and supports those who use the resources through training programmes.

Email: info@scriptureunion.org.uk
Internet: www.scriptureunion.org.uk

ISBN 1 85999 599 3

British Library Cataloguing-in-Publication Data
A catalogue record for this book is available from the British Library.

Cover design: Mark Carpenter Design Consultants
Cover photographs: Steve Shipman
Illustrations: Eira Reeves
Cover printed: Ebenezer Baylis & Son Ltd, The Trinity Press, Worcester
Internal pages printed and bound: Interprint, Malta

Contents

Introduction

Welcome to Glitter and Glue 5
What's so cool about craft? 5
Getting organised 6
Craft cupboard checklist 8
A cupboard full of crafts 9

All about God

Umbrella (God protects me) 12
The world (God made the world) 13
Comet (God made everything) 14
Tambourine (God loves praise) 15
Pop-up flower (God never changes) 15
Jigsaw
(Nothing is too difficult for God) 16
Lantern (God made the light) 16
Space (God made the universe) 17
Feet (God has plans for me) 18
Rainbow (God keeps his promises) 18
Watering can (God gives us water) 19
Melon (God is good to us) 20
Clouds (God made the clouds) 21
Fort (God is strong) 22
Humpty Dumpty (God helps me) 23

All about me

You're a star (I'm not grumpy) 24
Mirror (I'm beautiful) 24
Hiding place (God is looking after me) 25
My body (Look what I can do) 26
Mask (God gave me eyes to see) 27
I'm special (You know I am!) 27
All about me (I am wonderfully made) 28
Bedroom picture (God keeps me safe) 28
Telephone (I can talk to God) 29
Trumpet (I can make music) 30
Pillowcase (I'm sleepy) 30

Me (This is what I look like) 31
Lost sheep (I am lost without God) 31
Gift bag (I love to give presents) 32
Hat (Listen to adults) 32
Stick family (Me and my family) 33

I like food

Hungry (God gives us food) 34
Bread (We should say thank you) 34
Cake (I can share) .35
Cress (I am a gardener) 35
Pineapple
(God gives good things to eat) 36
Fruit bowl (God gives us fruit) 37
Honey pot (God keeps his promises) 38

My world

Today (What a wonderful day) 39
Windmill (God controls the wind) 40
Seasons (Our changing world) 41
Moon (God made the moon) 42
House (Building a house) 42
Snail (What's the time?) 43
Star (God made the stars) 44
Sun (God made the sun) 45
Tree (A home for the birds) 46
Roses (Flowers for Mum) 47
Flower (How beautiful!) 47
Summer and winter
(God gives us seasons) 48
Sunglasses (It's summer time) 49
Leaves (Autumn fun) 50
Snow (It's cold outside) 50
It's raining (Well, it often is!) 51

Special days

Christmas window .52

Glitter and Glue

Christmas stocking 53
Christmas card 54
Christingle 55
Valentine card 55
Hearts (Valentine's Day) 56
Mothering Sunday card 56
Easter card 57
Father's Day card 58
Farm (Harvest) 59
Rocket (5 November or other celebration with
fireworks) 60
Poppy (Remembrance Sunday) 61

The animals and the fish

Frog (I can sing) 61
Ant (Work hard) 62
Elephant (I can listen) 63
Pig (God made farm animals) 64
Sheep (I belong to God) 65
Cow (God owns all the animals) 66
Lion (I'm not scared) 67
Spider's web (You're big; I'm little) 67
Camel (God is amazing) 68
Caterpillar (I can change) 69
Tortoise (Everything belongs to God) 69
Cocoon (I am changing) 70
Butterfly (I am beautiful) 71
Giraffe (God made the wild animals) 72
The sea (God made the ocean) 73
Fish (I can be a fisherman) 74
Octopus (God is amazing) 75

The birds

Dove (I like peace: I like quiet) 76
Fan-tail dove (Noah sent out a dove) 77
Duck (God keeps me safe) 78
Ostrich (What am I good at?) 79
Penguin (We are all made by God) 80
Owl (A wise old bird) 81

Pelican (God made the birds) 82

Who is Jesus?

Cross (Jesus is alive) 83
Crown (Jesus is King) 84
Newsletter
(Jesus brings us good news) 84

More things to make

Thumb pot (I can be a potter) 85
Light (God gives us light to see) 85
Necklace (Say nice things) 86
Candle (No more darkness) 86
Handprint (Clap and sing to God) 87
Building (I can build) 87
Hula skirt (I can dance) 88
Cymbals (I can praise God) 88

Appendices

Bible index 89
Theme index 91

Introduction

Welcome to Glitter and Glue

For over four years now I have been running Toddler Groups. We have been having great fun with our toddlers, producing some of the crafts described within these pages.

The groups have been church-based, with the majority of our families from the local community, but not from the church. The parents have been pleased and proud of their children's efforts, and the look of sheer joy on the children's faces as they are praised is beautiful. One morning, about six months after we first started, I was approached by a mum who said she had a problem with the crafts. 'This is it,' I thought, 'she is going to object to us writing a Bible verse on the craft.' To my amazement and delight, her problem was that she had run out of room on her kitchen cabinets to display her child's work. She didn't want to take any down to make room for the new ones! For her and others the Bible verse was not a problem, instead it made the craft special. A craft that a child does in a toddler or similar group may well be the first thing they have ever produced, and as such will be precious. In my loft is a box of my children's artwork that I can't bear to throw away. I am sure it is the same for most parents.

What's so cool about craft?

Young children have an amazing capacity to learn. They are growing at a tremendous rate and absorb information like sponges. Using craft is a positive way of helping a child to develop co-ordination and grow in confidence. Whilst working with a child, any adult – leader, parent, guardian or carer – will notice that the relationship between the two blossoms. Shy children who will not leave their mother for anything else will come alone to the craft table to make something for that parent.

When I introduced crafts at our toddler group, my aim was to introduce the Word of God into family life. Each craft is based on a Bible verse, and the verse is written on the craft. In this way the craft becomes a gentle reminder of principles for living, of a promise of God, or of the way to God. Many people feel the Bible has nothing relevant to say to today's modern society. I wanted to show that God does have something to say concerning many aspects of contemporary living. The Bible is the living Word of God, not just an old book, and God wants to help us as we live our lives. At the same time, the Bible was not written for under-fives: the concepts and vocabulary are frequently beyond their stage of development and understanding and we are not expecting them to be able to read the words on their crafts. These are joint activities for an adult and child to do and use together. While the child is busy with card and glue, the adult is absorbing the words: in their own ways, both will be thinking God-thoughts. During the making time and when the item is on display at home, there will be occasions for explaining the words and talking about the meaning.

Each craft idea has a 'talkabout' suggestion to go with it and I have tried to keep these as simple as possible. Small children will not always understand why they are doing a particular craft or what the meaning may be. More often than not they will only be interested in what they are making. Try writing a few words of explanation on a card and placing it on your craft table for the adults to see. We are working on different levels here, introducing children and adults to the Word of God.

We are all made in the image of God. God gave us creativity, and made us all able to create, young and old. The aim is to give the child something that he/she is able to work on without causing frustration. Some of the crafts in the book do not appear to have a lot for the child to do. However, it takes them a long time to do a little. One- to two-year-olds just love to work with their 'Peter Pointer' fingers; pushing down stickers, finger-painting; that's when they have the most fun. We are not expecting the craft to look wonderful in adult terms: it is wonderful because they have made it! Getting it 'right' should not be our aim; it's not the end result we are interested in. The doing, the making, the sense of involvement and pleasure in creating are what matter most, as well as the feelings of achievement and the look of pleasure that says, 'I made this.'

So much is going on when we're 'doing' craft. Imagine a group of children sitting at a table playing with play dough and cutters. What do you see? They are pressing dough, rolling it out, pulling, moulding and shaping it. But what else is happening that you don't see? They are learning social skills as they sit together and share a limited amount of equipment; they are making choices; they are finding out the scientific nature of the materials; their physical skills are developing and their dexterity increasing as they manipulate tools and dough. They chat to each other so their communication and language are growing; they may be expressing how they are feeling emotionally by smoothing or thumping the material; their knowledge is expanding; their creativity is blossoming; their spiritual life can be stimulated – and all by a few minutes with a lump of dough!

Young children can have an active relationship with God. It is possible for them to understand that God loves them. This is the age when they begin to grasp the concepts of sharing, friendship, trust and security. We can help them to learn about God and how he wants them to know him. Simple Bible truths taught now, will become basic life principles.

Introduction

Being original!

I have tried to be original in this book in the treatment of the craft itself, and in the way it has been linked to the Bible. However, as you look through, you will notice some old favourites such as the lantern. I am not sure if anyone now knows who had the original idea, but if it was you, thank you very much: you have brought joy to many thousands of children. So many ideas are sparked by something we see around us, or are offshoots of other work we have seen at some time. If a craft in the book is similar to something you have done, I apologise, but there are only a few ways of doing a Valentine or Easter card, for example, and I have tried to use the most familiar images for the children in this age group. As you use this book, if you have an idea of how to adapt a craft so that it would be better suited to your group, then go ahead; have fun; be original!

I would like to thank my good friend Rachel, who got me started on all this by giving me a couple of ideas and some templates. Well done, Rach!

Annette Oliver.

GETTING ORGANISED

Laying out your room

How you organise your craft area will depend very much on the facilities you have at your group. Whether it is a toddler group with other play areas, or in a crèche with a limited space, there are some basic principles to follow.

If there is other activity in the room, your craft area should be at one end, or to the side of the room, not in the middle.

You will need a table for the children to sit or stand at, to carry out the craft. (See below for advice on covers.)

Do not try to fit too many children round the table at the same time. Repeat the activity with another small group, rather than crowding.

It's a good idea to have a separate table or area near by, for keeping your materials. This will avoid clutter on your table. You will be able to maintain better control if the children are given one item at a time.

Have a space available to put the completed work to dry. Most nurseries use an art rack to dry their work; however, these can be expensive. You may have someone who is able to make one for your group, or perhaps you could use a washing line and pegs. If space is not an issue, place the work in another room to dry.

General equipment

Keep your equipment and materials in a cupboard on the premises, if possible. If not, stacking plastic boxes make a good alternative and may be transported easily.

Limited funding is the usual situation so think carefully about your shopping list: you may be able to link up with other groups and buy in bulk.

Covers. Ideally site your craft table where the floor can be swept or washed easily. If this is not possible, make table covers from PVC-covered cloth (from fabric shops). You could have separate ones for different types of activity, eg play dough, painting, food preparation. Similar covers can be made for the floor, or use newspaper and throw it away each time. Roll the covers for storage. Cheap plastic sheeting should be used when working with clay, as it is easier to throw the sheet away than to try to clean it up. Spread floor covers flat when in use, to avoid tripping, and secure the edges with masking tape. If possible, wear shoes with grip, like trainers.

PVA glue and glue sticks. PVA (also known as 'school glue' or 'white glue') is used when the material you are working with is more difficult to secure. It is cost-effective, especially when bought in bulk from a DIY shop. Use glue sticks for lightweight fixing; they are easy for little hands to handle and reduce the mess considerably. It is essential that you check all glue is non-toxic, and suitable for your age group.

Safety scissors. There is nothing more frustrating than scissors that will not cut. It is worth investing in a few pairs of good safety scissors with a proper cutting edge and rounded ends. Remember to have scissors suitable for children who are left-handed as well as the standard right-handed type. Children from two-and-a-half upwards can be shown how to manipulate the scissors safely and guided to use them effectively. Don't push them too soon if their co-ordination in this area is still developing.

Paint and paintbrushes. Use washable poster paint, again age-specific for your group. The primary colours, red, yellow and blue, can be used to make other colours, ie red and yellow make orange; red and blue make purple; blue and yellow make green. Unless you intend to paint each week a large ready-mixed bottle of each will last a long time. Paintbrushes should be fairly chunky and the handles not too long.

Easels. It would be good to have one or two double-sided easels. These need not be expensive if you buy the very basic kind. Alternatively, you may have someone who is able to make them for you. It is much easier and less messy to paint at an easel but if this is not possible then a covered table is fine. You could use newspaper or a wipe-clean plastic cloth to protect the tables.

Aprons. In an ideal world we would all love to have brightly coloured plastic aprons with long cuffed sleeves.

If that is possible, then great. If not, an old shirt makes a very good alternative. The shirt should be no bigger than for a child aged five or six; otherwise it will be too big. Put the shirt on back to front and button it up. Do up the cuffs and turn them up to the right length, so that they are not flapping around.

Non-spill paint pots. These are inexpensive and can be found at many craft or toy shops.

Crayons. It is well worth investing in some good quality chunky crayons. They won't break in the children's hands and will last much longer than thin cheap ones.

Paper. Lining paper is good for painting. Cut lengths in advance and lay them under some books to make sure they are flat. Sugar paper is a good option as it is cheap and colourful. It can also be used in some of the other crafts. A4 card is recommended for most crafts in this book: try not to go smaller. Children enjoy large-scale work and can be discouraged if the work is always too small or fiddly. Card can be expensive if you buy it in small quantities. It is possible to buy in bulk from stationery catalogues, or office stores. Check to see if you have a paper factory with a shop in your area. This is the best way of buying any kind of paper as they often sell leftover products very cheaply. Tissue paper and crêpe paper are reasonably inexpensive and are very useful.

Collage materials. These can be collected by members of your team, family and friends, at little or no cost: odds of yarn and fabric; sweet papers and foil cake-cups; pasta shapes; wrapping paper and magazines; cereal boxes, and other large pieces of cardboard, egg boxes, yoghurt pots, insides of kitchen rolls, etc. Most things can be of use.

Be safe

Some precautions to avoid accidents and promote good standards.

Collage. It is important to avoid the use of very small items such as seeds. They can be swallowed, pushed into ears or up noses.

Pens. Remove pen tops and put them away while pens are in use, remembering to put them on again afterwards. Under-fives should have access to pens only when writing in a card with an adult. I would avoid using pens and pencils at all other times. A small child could easily damage an eye or choke on an unventilated top.

Cookery. It is not feasible to cook with under-fives in a large group setting. One-to-one supervision is preferable. Non-cook cookery is always popular: making fridge cakes, crispy cakes or decorating previously baked buns and biscuits. Be aware of hygiene rules and the possibility of food allergies. This applies to refreshments for children and adults too.

Spills. Wipe up any spills immediately. Have an old towel available to dry the area after you have wiped up the liquid. This reduces the risk of someone slipping.

Building issues. Check that the premises have had a safety audit and that all regulations have been met, also that your group is covered by insurance.

Child protection. Check on the church or local authority policy in your area and make sure your group complies.

What about staff?

Young children need good supervision and plenty of it! It is advisable to have one adult for every two children aged two-and-a-half to four. A child under two-and-a-half usually needs one-to-one supervision. It actually depends upon individual children, how independent they are and their capabilities. If you are limited in the help you have, ask the parent/carer to sit with their child. Another option is to limit the number of children present at the craft table. Four would be the maximum for two adults.

Expectations

As far as the child is concerned, it is the process of making-and-doing that is important, not the end result. You may have prepared an example of the finished item and their version is completely different. How will you react? What will you say? Does it matter whether they have done it 'right'? Craft activities are about pride in working and having a sense of achievement. But they are about so much more! Some three-year-olds may be capable of producing an exact replica of your example; some will not. Is it important that their elephant has two ears and a trunk or that children have made it themselves? It is possible to allow young children to complete a craft alone, by giving one item and one instruction at a time until they have finished. Children as young as ten months to a year can have fun, just by sitting with an adult and watching them stick down all the bits, with the child pushing them down with their fingers. As far as that child is concerned, 'I made it.' They may not be able to tell you in words but their expression will speak volumes; they will have had a great time and the one-to-one time spent with a caring adult is invaluable.

It's wonderful to have a fridge covered in masterpieces, but that isn't the main reason for trying crafts with young children: it's the exploring, the experimenting, the making and the togetherness that make 'craft' much more than a way to keep children occupied.

Funding

Whatever kind of group you run you will incur expenses. How will you fund your group? If it is church-based you may have been given a budget. If that is not

Introduction

the case there are other options. One is to charge a small fee for attending, all of which can be put back into running costs. Another option is to apply to local trusts or charities for a capital or running cost grant. Your local Voluntary Services should have a list of such trusts and guidelines on how to apply. A good way of collecting items you need is to put a specific list up on your notice board. In order to obtain good quality equipment, you will need to be very definite as to your requirements. It is important to say that you are looking for equipment that is 'as new'. Organising fund-raising events is a way of involving other people in your group. Consider inviting party-plan organisers who will sell, for instance, children's books or clothes and give your group commission on sales. It may seem a lot of extra work but the social benefits can be more than the amount of money raised.

How, when and where to use this book

Glitter and Glue is packed with ideas which have been used effectively in church toddler groups, crèches, Sunday school and holiday clubs but it can be used in many other situations where young children meet – or one-to-one at home. Once the materials have been prepared, each activity takes just a few minutes so it is ideal for a limited time or when start and finish times are flexible. In a group setting, the craft table could be a regular feature, with a few children taking turns to make their items. Or use *Glitter and Glue* for dip-in ideas when you need to extend a programme or want an activity particularly geared to younger children. Some of the crafts are suitable for children aged up to ten and have been used effectively in an after-school club for that age group. With older children you will not need to do as much preparation as they will be able to complete the whole craft themselves, following a sample item.

How you use it is up to you – but we hope you and 'your' children will *enjoy* making and doing together.

> ### TIP
> When writing words on the craftwork, remember to use lower case and printed lettering. Only use a capital letter at the beginning of a sentence or for names and proper nouns.

Many of the following crafts use A4 card (approximately 29 x 21 cm). You can substitute scrap card (from packaging), stiff paper or sugar paper if required.

Craft shops and educational suppliers now sell 'chenille wires' instead of 'pipe cleaners': these come in various lengths, thicknesses and colours, including glittery ones.

Short flat wooden craft sticks (lolly sticks) come in many colours, and have rounded ends which makes them ideal for children to use and hold.

CRAFT CUPBOARD CHECKLIST

Basics

White paper
Coloured paper
White and coloured card
Sugar paper/large backing paper
Lining paper/long lengths
Crêpe paper
Wallpaper (but beware of ready-pasted as the paste often contains fungicide)
Chunky wax crayons
Colouring pencils
Pencils
Safety scissors (right- and left-handed)
Glue sticks
PVA glue and spreaders
Ready-mixed paint
Paintbrushes
Sponges
Shallow plastic trays
Old newspapers (checked for unsuitable pictures)
Cereal packets
Cardboard tubes
Large packaging boxes
Yoghurt pots
Egg boxes
Magazines with suitable pictures
Old greetings cards

Specials

Glitter pens
Glitter
Tinsel
Lametta strands
Chenille wires
Sequinned fabric scraps
Metallic card
Metallic foil
Tissue paper
Embossed wallpaper
Gift wrapping paper
Stickers
Wobbly eyes (self-adhesive)
Pinking or curved scissors
Felt-tipped pens
White and coloured chalk
Stampers and ink pads
Wooden spoons
Short plant support sticks
Short flat wooden craft sticks (lolly sticks)

Cotton wool
Natural materials (leaves, 'craft' feathers, cones, twigs)
Dried pasta shapes
Yarn, string, wool
Fabric scraps
Ribbon
Large buttons
Empty cotton reels

...and all those bits and pieces that will come in useful one day!

For your use only

Craft knife
Sharp scissors
Blu-tack
Sticky tape and dispenser
Paper masking tape
Hole punch
Ruler
Labels
Kitchen roll
Wet wipes
Tissues
Stapler and
staples
Staple
remover
Thick 'marker'
pen
Coloured gel
pens
Paper
fasteners
Paper clips
String
Paper crimper
Plastic spoons
(for stirring or
ladling paint,
glue, etc)
Clothes pegs

A CUPBOARD FULL OF CRAFTS

Glitter and Glue gives you 101 craft 'makes' but there are many, many more you can try. Here are some ideas to extend your craft time – and create your own masterpieces in the process!

Cards: At special times of the year cards are an easy craft to make and use as a gift. It is always better to start with A4 card. The smaller the card the more difficult it is for the young child to work with. Vary the design by having the fold at the side or the top, by trimming the edges with shaped scissors or using unusual colours or shapes. Decorate with drawings, collage or sticky shapes: help children 'write' their names inside.

Clay: Working with clay is messy and needs thorough cleaning up but it is fantastic fun and well worth the effort. Use 'air hardening clay'. There are several on the market for this age group, and they are relatively inexpensive. Clay helps children to develop co-ordination and stimulates their imagination and creativity. Be generous with quantities so the children have something to really get to grips with. Give them total freedom and watch them surprise you. They will love the feel and texture and will be happy shaping and moulding without making anything recognisable! It will give good opportunities to chat and for relationship-building as you sit at the table. (See page 85 for making a thumb pot.)

Collage, cutting and sticking: Usually these are pictures made from a variety of materials (old greetings cards, fabric scraps, tissue paper, pasta, wrappers) stuck onto sugar paper or card. This may be abstract or planned to a theme. Many children will spend ages cutting pictures from old magazines and sticking them to sheets of paper! Another option is to use scrap pieces of A4 card to cut out shapes to form a picture. When working with a young age group it is better to keep things as simple as possible. Have most of your collage pieces pre-cut but let the older children do some for themselves. Individual collages are popular but group ones have the added bonus of working together and producing something much bigger than could be achieved alone.

Colouring: If using pre-drawn outlines, make sure they are clear, bold and large. Colouring is a good activity for developing skills and pencil control.

Cooking: Almost all children love to cook. Depending on the type of group you have and in what building, your insurance may restrict you in cooking with under-fives. But there is plenty of fun to be had with non-cook cookery (fridge cakes, crispy cakes, etc) or decorating pre-cooked fairy cakes or plain biscuits. Very small children will still see it as a great achievement even if it doesn't go into or come out of an oven. Make sure surfaces, equipment and hands are clean. Involve the children in washing up too (even if you have to do it again later!). Put the prepared food aside until the end of the session.

Dough (play dough, salt/baking dough): A dough table provides endless hours of interest, creativity and pleasure. It is relaxing, non-threatening and yet satisfying and exciting at the same time. Children love to have generous quantities of dough to handle. Here's a simple way to make dough quickly.

Play dough

You will need: 1.5 kg flour, 500 g salt, 400 ml water, large mixing bowl.

Mix everything together to make a dough.

If it comes out too sticky, provide children with plenty of

extra flour when playing with it. If it comes out too dry, splash on a little water as children play with the dough.

This is not an accurate dough recipe, but the variations in types of dough can be great fun in themselves. The type of flour used and even the weather can make dough vary greatly. The advantage of this recipe is that children can join in safely and do their own preparation (which is as much fun as 'real' cooking). **Salt or baking dough** feels similar to play dough but you can cook it to make durable models. Mix 300 g plain flour, 300 g salt, 15 ml cooking oil, 200 ml water in a large bowl (multiply the quantities for a large group of children). Add a little more water if the dough is too dry. Knead well on a floured surface until the dough has a smooth, springy texture. Cook the children's creations on a greased baking tray in a medium oven for 20–60 minutes.

Home-made dough will last for several uses if stored in a plastic bag in a container with a well-fitting lid.

Drawing: This is best done with chunky c rayons. Little hands can grip them well, which gives more co-ordination. It is possible to buy chunky crayons with shaped tops so that the slightly older children will have more control and will not be frustrated. Thinner crayons give better control but are easily broken. Crayons do not have a long life; they will need replacing from time to time. Use large sheets of paper so that children have freedom to create their own images.

Frieze, mural: For large-scale craft with a group of children, fix long strips of paper around a wall and paint or collage along them. This can be abstract or to a theme. For instance, you could have a field with trees and plants growing through the seasons, or a crowd of people, or sheep following a shepherd. Children also love 'painting' with water on an outside wall.

Glue pictures: For abstract or themed pictures, draw a shape in glue on the background paper; sprinkle on glitter, sand, wood-shavings, or press on scrunched tissue to make a picture. Shake off excess and then put glue on another section and repeat.

Junk modelling: All your left-over bits and pieces can be used in model making. Cartons, pots and boxes are very useful. Don't throw anything away! Paper masking tape should be used with PVA glue to fix the models, as it can be painted. Prepare an example or two to show the children (or better still, sit alongside them and make your own models) but leave them free to create. You will end up with some amazing structures. If the children will be painting the models themselves, they may not be dry enough to take home. Consider painting the boxes yourself beforehand to avoid this problem.

Mobiles: Children love to have them hung in their bedroom, and will enjoy making them. Coat hangers make cheap and easy frames to hang strings of all sorts of items: card shapes, shells, dried clay pieces. Only the eldest and most capable in your group will be able to thread the elements onto the string. Even they will possibly have a difficult time tying them on. It is advisable to prepare the hanger in advance. Once the child has decorated the elements to hang from the mobile, sit with him/her to tie them on. They will enjoy seeing the finished product come together.

Montage, mosaics: Cut out lots of small pictures and put them together on a backing to make a larger picture. Or cut and tear scraps to give an abstract mosaic effect.

Painting, finger-painting: Some adults have a fear of painting, owing to the potential for mess but it doesn't have to be messy at all. Even one-year-olds have a great time if supervised. Parents will always be willing to get involved, as this is something many children don't do at home. Cover the table, the floor and the artists, use non-spill paint pots, use an easel where possible, have plenty of adult supervision (one adult per two children) and have warm water, cloths and a towel to hand for clearing up afterwards. When finger-painting, aim to have one adult per child. The children can either dab their fingers in the paint and then draw on the paper, or, if you have a washable surface, put the paint direct on to the table, let the child draw in it and then press a piece of paper over the paint to print a picture.

Papier-mâché: To make papier-mâché dilute PVA glue 50:50 with water. Rip newspaper into strips about 2.5 cm wide. Dip the paper into the glue and squeeze off excess glue between finger and thumb. Lay the paper strips onto the base. Work one layer at a time. In an ideal world you would allow one layer to dry before putting on the next layer; working with small children at home this would be possible. In a large group setting split the activity over two sessions. Complete the papier-mâché in the first session. This will leave a long drying period. Then decorate in the second session.

Printing: Use paint and sponge shapes, potatoes or fingertips. Experiment with leaves, cut fruit, bark, netting, textured fabric, corrugated card – anything reasonably flat can give a print. Put the paint into shallow trays and use one colour at a time so that you don't end up with everything mud-coloured. With fabric paint use sponge and stencils. Put a sheet of cardboard under the fabric to absorb excess and avoid paint soaking through to the other side. This can be a lot of fun. Once again, because there is not a great amount of paint out at any one time, mess can be kept to a minimum.

Puppets: Make all sorts of puppets from bits and pieces. Cut out a shape (person, animal, whatever) from card, tape a short stick to the back and you have a puppet! Or add buttons or felt features to socks or gloves; draw a face or body on a plain paper bag; draw a face on the bowl of a wooden spoon, and wrap a piece of fabric round the handle; wrap strips of paper round fingers, or decorate cardboard tubes. Improvise a theatre from a cardboard box and you will be amazed at the productions even very young children concoct together.

Rubbings: Lay a piece of thin-but-strong paper over a

textured surface and rub with a wax crayon held sideways. Watch the pattern appear. Dark-coloured crayons show up best. Use a little paper masking tape to hold the paper and the item below steady while the child works. You can buy textured templates, but use other everyday materials: corrugated card, netting, embossed wallpaper and fabrics.

Sewing: Punch holes round the edges of old greetings cards or shaped card templates. Bind the end of a piece of string or wool with sticky tape to make a 'needle'. Tie a large knot in the other end or tape it to the 'wrong' side of the card: let the children sew in and out of the holes.

Stencils and templates: You can buy stencils and templates or make your own. If you draw a shape onto thick card and cut it out carefully with a craft knife, you can make both a stencil and a template at the same time. (If you cut them out of a good quality ice cream or margarine container, you will have wipe-clean ones.) For young children, hold the stencil and paper steady with paper masking tape or Blu-tack. Let them paint or sponge-print over the top. Templates can be traced round to get a shape to cut out or colour; you can also keep the template in place and paint over the top so you get a silhouette when the template is removed.

Symmetrical shapes: Fold a piece of paper in half, open out, put paint on one side; fold over again and press down. Open up the paper to see a mirror image.

Things to wear: This includes hats, necklaces, masks, badges, etc. There are just a few basic principles to follow depending on what you make: use strong thread or shirring elastic for a necklace; make sure there are no sharp objects; use paper clips to secure badges; cover ends of staples with sticky tape so the points don't catch in hair or on skin.

Wax resist: Draw a picture using a wax candle on paper (choose the same colour candle as the paper). Mix up paint with extra water. With a large brush, paint all over the paper and watch as the hidden picture is revealed. Children love doing this themselves or you can prepare surprise pictures for them.

UMBRELLA

Verse

You have been a shelter for me, O God.
(Psalm 61:3 paraphrase)

You will need: A4 card in various colours including blue; acetate; marker pen; scissors.
Each child will need: Sheet of blue A4 card; umbrella template; raindrops; sun; rainbow; crayons; glue stick.

Your preparation

Write the verse across the top of the sheet of blue card. Cut out raindrops from the acetate. Cut the sun, umbrella and rainbow shapes from the card.

What to do

Colour in the rainbow. Glue the umbrella, sun, rainbow and raindrops to the blue card. Make sure the umbrella is towards the base of the card.

Talkabout

God can protect us from harm, and has told us in the Bible that if we follow him, he will keep this promise.

THE WORLD

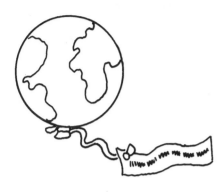

Verse

The world and its people belong to God.
(Psalm 24:1 paraphrase)

You will need: Green crêpe paper; continent templates (enlarge the templates below on a photocopier); A4 card; marker pen; scissors; balloon weights (obtainable from fancy-dress shops etc); string.
Each child will need: A blue helium-filled balloon (with string attached); continents; glue stick; verse on strip of card.

Your preparation

Cut the continents out of green crêpe paper. Make a banner out of a 5 cm-wide strip of card and write the verse on one side and the child's name on the other. Make a hole in one end for the string.

What to do

Glue one side of all the continents first, and then attach them to the balloon. Tie the banner onto the end of the string.

Talkabout

God made the world. It belongs to him. He made it for us to live in and we belong to him too.

> ### TIP
> Each balloon should come with string attached. You will need to tie a weight onto the string so that the child can work with it at the right level. You may need to enlist the help of parents/carers this week. Don't let go of the string when you're outside! And if you meet in a building with a high ceiling, make sure the string is long enough to reach if the balloon floats away.

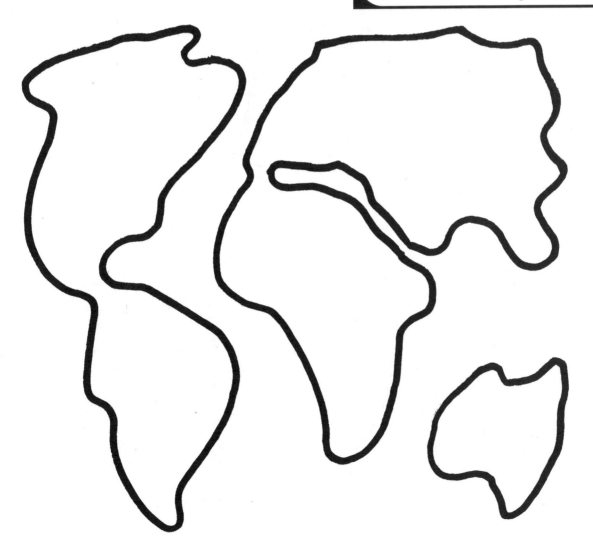

COMET

Verse

I, God, will show my wonders in heaven above. (Acts 2:19 paraphrase)

You will need: Black A4 card; silver A4 card; comet template; silver gel pen; scissors.
Each child will need: Black A4 card; black houses and tower blocks; a silver comet; glue stick; glitter pen; chalk.

Your preparation

With the gel pen write the verse at the top of the black background card. From another sheet of black card cut out houses and tower blocks. Using the silver card cut out the comet.

What to do

Glue down a row of houses and tower blocks to make a town. Then glue the comet into the sky. Outline the comet with the glitter pen. Using the chalk, draw little squares on the houses to show light at the windows.

Talkabout

God made stars and everything in the sky. Look at the sky when it is dark. See how beautiful it is. Just think how powerful God is.

TAMBOURINE

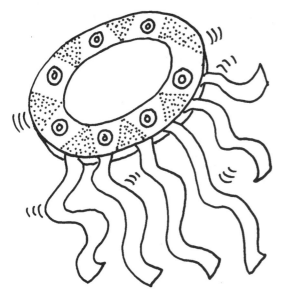

Verse

God is great and worthy of praise. (Psalm 96:4 paraphrase)

You will need: Crêpe paper in various colours; paper plates; rice or lentils; small envelopes; marker pen; scissors; stapler.
Each child will need: 2 paper plates; an envelope of rice or lentils; sticky shapes; glue stick; glitter pens; crayons; crêpe paper streamers; PVA glue and spreader.

Your preparation

Cut the crêpe paper into long streamers. With the marker pen write the verse on the back of each plate on the outside edge. Place enough rice or lentils inside a small envelope to make a good rattling noise.

What to do

Glue both inside edges of each plate with the PVA glue. At one side place the end of a few streamers, and in the middle place an envelope of rice or lentils. Then place the second plate on top of the first, trapping the streamers and envelope inside. At this point an adult should staple both plates together. Now the child is free to decorate the tambourine.

Talkabout

God is amazing and we should praise him. We can use music and song to say thank you to God for all the wonderful things he does for us.

Idea

Put some joyful children's music on and encourage the children to use their tambourines.

POP-UP FLOWER

Verse

Flowers and grass fade away, but what our God has said will never change. (Isaiah 40:8)

You will need: Yellow A4 card; sticky labels; crêpe paper; you could use the petal template on page 47; marker pen; scissors/pruning shears.
Each child will need: A disposable cup; a wooden barbecue skewer; 2 yellow circles 3 cm in diameter; crêpe paper petals; glue stick; a label; crayons.

Your preparation

Cut the circles out of the yellow card. Fold the crêpe paper over so that you have a fourfold thickness. Cut out the petals. With the marker pen write the verse on the sticky labels. Make a hole in the bottom of each cup with the point of a skewer. Using pruning shears or sharp scissors cut the sharp tip off each skewer.

What to do

Draw a happy face on one yellow circle and a sad face on the other. Cover the reverse of each yellow circle with glue. Place the edges of the petals all around one circle to make up the flower. Place one end of the skewer in the centre of the circle and cover with the other yellow circle. Put the label on the outside of the cup. Push the stick down into the cup so that the flower can pop up and down.

Talkabout

God will never break a promise. We can depend on God always to be loving and kind.

All about God

JIGSAW

Verse

With people it's impossible, but not with God.
(Mark 10:27 paraphrase)

You will need: White A4 card; marker pen; scissors; fish template (enlarge the template on page 74 on a photocopier).
Each child will need: Thick white A4 card with a big fish on; crayons.

Your preparation

Photocopy or copy the fish design onto one side of the card. On the other side write the verse.

What to do

Let children colour the fish and decorate the other side of the card with colour in any way they choose. When they have finished cut the card up into two, four or six wavy pieces depending on the age and skill of the child. They then have a jigsaw to take home. Before you begin to cut the picture, explain to the child what you are going to do and why. If they object, leave the picture whole.

Talkabout

Sometimes we find things hard to do, just like a jigsaw puzzle. God can do anything. Nothing is too hard for God.

LANTERN

Verse

God said, 'I command light to shine!' And light started shining. (Genesis 1:3)

You will need: Marker pen; scissors; newspaper; card for handles; A4 card; stapler.
Each child will need: Sheet of A4 card; a card handle; sticky tape; safety scissors; PVA glue and spreader; glitter.

Your preparation

Cut enough handles for each lantern and write the verse on one side. Fold each child's A4 sheet of card in half lengthways. Make cuts 8 cm long and 2 cm apart, all the way along the card. Ensure you make the incisions at the fold.

What to do

Older children may wish to try the cutting themselves, so use safety scissors. Open up the card and dot PVA glue onto one side. Make sure the newspaper is under the card, then sprinkle glitter onto the glue and shake it off again. The newspaper will catch the excess glitter which you can then re-use. Bend the card round to form the shape of the lantern. An adult should staple the lantern top and bottom. Stick the handle on the top using sticky tape; ensure the verse is visible. Allow to dry.

Talkabout

God made the light so that we could see.

SPACE

Statement

God made space.

You will need: *A4 card; moon template; thread; marker pen; scissors; hole punch.*
Each child will need: *2 circles, 20 cm in diameter; a crescent moon, 20 cm from tip to tip; green, blue, yellow and white tissue paper; glue stick.*

Your preparation

Cut the thread into 15 cm lengths, 4 for each child. Cut out the card circles. One circle will be the earth, the other the sun. Make triangular cuts into the outside edge of the sun to give it a better shape. Cut out the crescent moons. Cut rectangles 10 cm x 4 cm and write the statement in marker pen on them. Punch a hole in the top of each rectangle, and in the top and bottom of each earth, sun and moon.

What to do

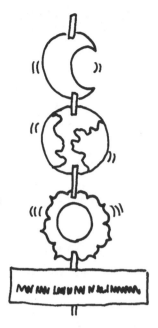

Tear off bits of tissue paper and scrunch them up. Stick white onto the moon, yellow onto the sun, and green and blue onto the earth with the glue stick. When each child has finished, tie thread onto the top and bottom of the moon. Then tie the bottom thread to the earth. Tie thread onto the bottom of the earth to attach the sun, and the same to the sun to attach the statement. You then have a wall hanging of the earth, moon and sun in space.

Talkabout

God made the world for us to live in. He made the sun and moon to give us light. God is always looking after us.

All about God

FEET

Verse

God decides where we will go and what will happen to us. (Proverbs 20:24 paraphrase)

You will need: A4 card in various colours including white; marker pen; scissors; foot template.
Each child will need: several 'feet'; glue stick; crayons; sheet of white A4 card.

Your preparation

Using the template cut enough feet for each child to have several. Write the verse at the top of the white A4 card.

What to do

Encourage the child to stick the feet down onto the card, all facing the same way as if they were walking along a path. Then, with the crayons, draw the pathway and colour all around.

Talkabout

God has a good plan for our lives.

RAINBOW

Verse

The rainbow that I, God, have put in the sky will remind you that I will keep this promise for ever. (Genesis 9:13 paraphrase)

You will need: Tissue paper; circle template 19 cm in diameter; circle template 9 cm in diameter; black marker pen; A4 acetate.
Each child will need: A4 acetate; strips of tissue paper in rainbow colours; PVA glue and spreader.

Your preparation

Draw the rainbow onto the acetate using the circle templates and marker pen. Write the verse along the bottom of the acetate. Cut the tissue paper into strips about 1 cm wide.

What to do

Using PVA glue, coat the inside of the rainbow, then stick the tissue strips on in order. From outside: red, orange, yellow, green, blue, indigo, violet. Allow to dry.

Talkabout

God made a promise never to flood the whole earth again. He made the rainbow so that when we see it in the sky, we will remember God's promise.

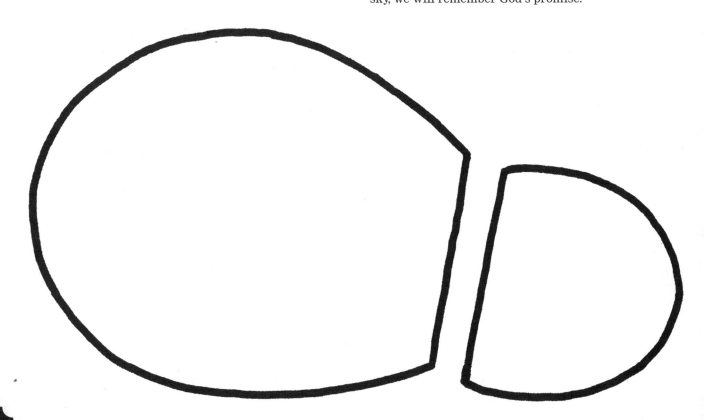

WATERING CAN

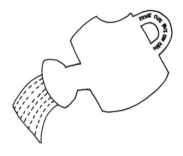

Statement

God gives us water.

You will need: Yellow A4 card; coloured A4 card; acetate; watering can and flower template (enlarge the templates below on a photocopier); marker pen; scissors.
Each child will need: 2 watering cans; flowers; acetate water; glue stick; crayons.

Your preparation

Using the template and the yellow card, cut out 2 watering cans for each child. Cut the acetate into arch shapes, and with a permanent marker draw lines of dashes on to it to suggest pouring water. Using various colours cut flowers out of card. Write the verse on each side of the handle of the watering can.

What to do

Glue the two watering cans together, trapping the water at the spout. Decorate the can with the flowers and crayons.

Talkabout

We use water to wash, to drink, to splash and have fun. God sends the rain to give us all the water we need.

Idea

If you are doing this craft in summer, perhaps you could have a water playtime outside. Little plastic watering cans are great fun in water play.

> **TIP**
>
> Be safe: Always supervise water play and never leave the water unattended. Remind parents/carers to put sunblock and protective hats on the children.

MELON

Verse

The earth is full of the goodness of God. (Psalm 33:5 paraphrase)

You will need: Green and pink A4 card; black marker pen; scissors; ball of string; arm and leg template.
Each child will need: Large green semi-circle; smaller pink semi-circle; 2 arms and 2 legs; 2 wiggly eyes (self-adhesive ones available in craft shops) and 4 paper fasteners; glue stick; black crayon; loop of string.

Your preparation

With the green and pink card cut out the semi-circles, making the green slightly larger to make a rind on the melon. Write the verse on what will be the green rind of the melon. Using the left-over bits of card cut out pink arms and green feet. Make a hole in each of these for the fastener to go through. Make corresponding holes in the green card, along the rind. Cut 8 cm lengths of string to make a loop to hang the melon.

What to do

Put the loop at the top of the green semi-circle, ie in the middle of the straight side. Stick down the pink semi-circle, trapping the loop. Next attach the arms and legs with the fasteners. Using the glue stick again, put on the eyes. Encourage the child to draw the nose, mouth and freckles on the melon with the black crayon.

Talkabout

All the good things on the earth are made by God.

CLOUDS

Verse

When I send clouds, and a rainbow appears, I will remember my promise. (Genesis 9:14–15 paraphrase)

You will need: White A4 card; cloud templates (enlarge the templates below on a photocopier); scissors; marker pen; ball of thread; hole punch.
Each child will need: 4 weather clouds; 2 chenille wires; 5 lengths of thread; crayons; PVA glue and spreader; silver glitter; newspaper.

Your preparation

Cut card strips 2 cm wide and 20 cm long; punch a hole in one end and write the verse in marker pen on both sides. Cut out the cloud templates and punch a hole in the top of each. For younger children, make the hanging frame in advance. Thread the verse onto the middle of one wire. Then twist the two wires together in the middle and spread the wires to form the shape of a cross. Hang different lengths of thread from each wire and tie one in the middle to hang the mobile from the ceiling.

What to do

Children should colour their weather clouds, then use the PVA glue and glitter to produce some kind of silver lining! Dot the glue around and spread the glitter, shaking off the excess onto the newspaper. Older children can have a go at making the hanger as above and tying the clouds onto the hanger.

Talkabout

God's promise was never to flood the whole earth again. When it's stormy or raining, look for the rainbow and remember God's promise.

All about God

FORT

Verse

You are my fortress, my place of safety; you are my God, and I trust you. (Psalm 91:2)

You will need: A4 card; marker pen; scissors; fort template (enlarge the template below on a photocopier). *Each child will need:* A fort; small square sponge; small amount of paint in flat trays; apron.

Your preparation

Photocopy and enlarge the fort template onto A4 card with the door in the middle. Cut out the arch of the doorway, so that the door will fold down like a drawbridge. With the marker pen write the verse on the inside of the door so that it can be read when you pull the door down. Draw a few small slit windows on the fort.

What to do

Encourage children to sponge-paint the bricks onto the walls of the fort, using the small sponges and paint. They can go anywhere and any way up; just have fun.

Talkabout

We know that forts and castles are strong houses. If we lived there we would be safe. Nothing is stronger than God. When we trust him to look after us, we will be very safe.

HUMPTY DUMPTY

Verse

When someone stumbles or falls, you, God, give a helping hand. (Psalm 145:14)

You will need: A4 card; scraps of material; black marker pen; scissors; Humpty picture (enlarge the picture below on a photocopier).
Each child will need: Humpty Dumpty picture on A4 card; scraps of material; crayons; PVA glue and spreader.

Your preparation

Photocopy and enlarge the picture of Humpty onto card. With the marker pen write the verse at the top of the card. Cut the scraps of material into small pieces.

What to do

With the PVA glue and scraps, dress Humpty. Colour the rest of the picture.

Talkabout

When we have a problem or we are in trouble, God is able to help us and keep us safe.

YOU'RE A STAR

Verse

Do everything without complaining so that you shine like a star. (Philippians 2:14–15 paraphrase)

You will need: Sheets of A3 card; sheets of A4 card; star template (photocopy and enlarge the template on page 44); marker pen; scissors; stapler; sticky tape.
Each child will need: Headband; star; glitter shapes; glue stick.

Your preparation

With the A3 card long side uppermost, cut 4 cm-wide strips to be headbands. Using the template cut stars from the A4 card. Write the verse on the headbands with the marker pen, leaving room in the centre for the star and space at the ends to adjust for fit.

What to do

Let children decorate the headbands and stars with the glitter shapes, using the glue sticks. Glue stars into position in the middle of the headband. You could staple it to make it really secure, but tape over the ends of the staples so that they don't catch in hair. Try the headband round the child's head and staple the headband to fit. Put aside to dry.

Talkabout

God loves us all the time, no matter how we feel. Sometimes we may feel grumpy or sad; sometimes we feel happy. Whether we are at home, school, or at a friend's, try to do everything with a smile and not with a grumpy face.

MIRROR

Statement

I am special to God.

You will need: Permanent marker; pen; ruler; bowl of warm water, face cloths and towel; cheap but safe mirrors.
Each child will need: A mirror; tile grout; glass pebbles or beads; apron.

Your preparation

Using the ruler mark a border around the edges of the mirror, at least 2–3 cm wide, but appropriate to the size of the mirror. Write the statement above the border at what will be the bottom of the mirror.

What to do

Help children to put the grout around the edge of the mirror, up to the pre-marked border. Then push the pebbles or beads into the grout to decorate the mirror.

Talkabout

God loves you very much. He made you and thinks you look great. He loves the colour of your hair and eyes, and thinks you have a lovely smile. Take a look!

HIDING PLACE

Verse

God, you are my hiding place; you keep me from trouble. (Psalm 32:7 paraphrase)

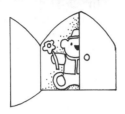

You will need: Templates for teddy, hat, waistcoat, eyes, nose and flower (enlarge the templates below on a photocopier); marker pen; scissors/craft knife; coloured A4 card; pencil.
Each child will need: 2 sheets of A4 card; teddy; hat and waistcoat; 2 eyes and a nose; flower; glue stick; crayons.

Your preparation

Draw a double door onto one of each pair of A4 sheets. With scissors/craft knife, cut along the bottom, across the top and down the middle of the door. Fold back sides so that the doors open. Using various colours of card, cut round teddy and other templates. Write the verse above the door. On the second A4 sheet draw pencil guidelines round the area visible when the door on the top sheet is opened.

What to do

Glue the hat, waistcoat, eyes and nose, onto the teddy and then glue teddy to the lower sheet, inside the pencilled guidelines. Draw a mouth on the teddy. Finally stick the cutaway door sheet to the bottom sheet of card.

Talkabout

We can always trust God to keep us safe and look after us.

Idea

If you wish, you could put a picture of the child behind the door to make this craft more personal. This requires prior planning. Take a camera to your group for a couple of weeks to make sure you get a photo of each child. Inform the parents of your plan and get permission to take the photos. Keep the photos safe at all times.

MY BODY

Verse

Our bodies have many parts. (1 Corinthians 12:14 paraphrase)

You will need: Templates of all the body parts (enlarge the templates below on a photocopier); hole punch; marker pen; scissors.
Each child will need: 1 head, 1 body; 2 arms, 2 legs; a short, smooth stick; PVA glue and spreader; paper fasteners; crayons.

Your preparation

Using templates and scissors cut out the number of bodies you need. Write the verse on the tummy of each body. Punch holes in the right places to attach arms, legs and head. Make up some bodies with the paper fasteners for the younger children.

What to do

Let the children put the bodies together and help them to insert paper fasteners; then draw on faces, hands, feet and clothes with crayons. Stick the trunk of the body to the stick as a handle. When the child jiggles the stick the body should move.

Talkabout

We are all made up of different parts: hands, feet, eyes, ears – and each part of our body has an important job to do. To keep our bodies healthy we should exercise, and eat healthy food.

Idea

If you have a scrap box, cut very small pieces of fabric for the children to stick down with PVA glue to dress the body.

> **TIP**
> Be careful – paper fasteners have sharp points.

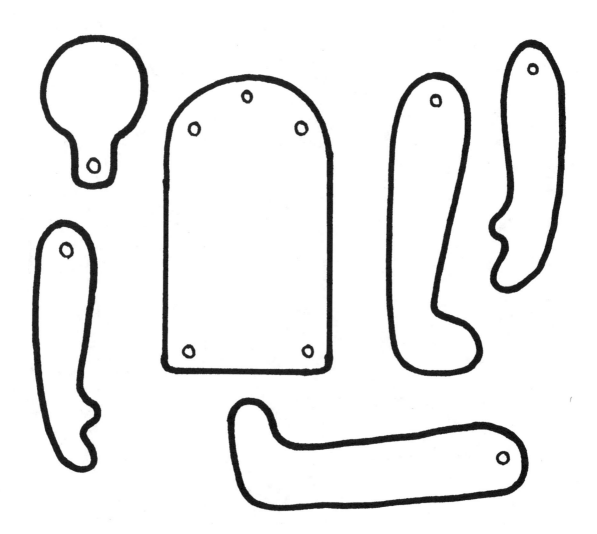

MASK

Statement

Thank you God for eyes to see.

You will need: Garden canes cut to 20 cm, sanded to remove splinters or flat wooden craft sticks (lolly sticks); black A4 card; mask template; sticky tape; silver gel pen; scissors/craft knife.
Each child will need: Eye-mask; garden cane or craft stick; feathers, glitter shapes, stars; glue stick.

Your preparation

Using the template, cut the eye-masks out of the black card. Write the verse along the top of the mask using the gel pen. Attach the stick to the back of the mask, at one side, with sticky tape.

What to do

With the glue stick attach the glitter shapes and stars to decorate the mask. Then glue the feathers to the mask on the same side as the stick, making them stick up into the air away from the mask itself.

Talkabout

God has made many beautiful things in our world. Say thank you to God for eyes to see trees, flowers, and the people who look after you.

I'M SPECIAL

Verse

God has even counted the hairs on your head, so don't be afraid. (Matthew 10:30–31 paraphrase)

You will need: White and skin-tone A4 card; marker pen; scissors; wool in yellow, brown, fawn, black, orange (to match hair colours).
Each child will need: Skin-tone circle 20 cm in diameter; wool for hair; card for eyes, mouth, nose, ears and hat shapes; PVA glue and spreader; crayons.

Your preparation

Draw and cut out skin-tone circles for the faces. Cut the wool into long and shorter lengths. Draw eyes, nose, ears, mouth and hat for each face and cut them out of the white card. With the marker pen write the verse on the hat.

What to do

Colour the mouth, eyes, nose, ears and hat. With the PVA glue let the child stick down all the bits onto the skin-tone circle to make a face. They should then choose the wool they wish to stick on as hair. The children should try to get the style similar to theirs.

Talkabout

God knows everything about us, even the number of hairs on our head. We are very special to God.

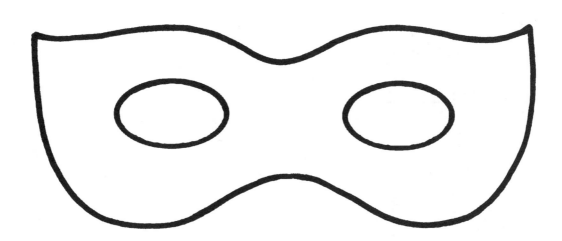

ALL ABOUT ME

Verse

I thank you God because of the wonderful way you made me. (Psalm 139:14 paraphrase)

You will need: *Sheets of A3 card; marker pen; ruler; old red lipsticks; antiseptic wet wipes; pencil.*
Each child will need: *Sheet of A3 card; crayons.*

Your preparation

With the marker pen write the verse across the top of the A3 card. Then write the following words: My eyes are (draw a big eye for the child to colour), my hair is (draw a box to colour), my lips are (leave a space), this is my hand, this is my foot (leave a large space).

What to do

First, draw around their hand and foot. Next put lipstick on their lips and have them kiss the page in the right place. Wipe the lipstick with an antiseptic wet wipe to make sure it is clean for the next child. Then let children colour their eye and hair boxes and their hands and feet if they wish. This is a keepsake so remember to write their names on neatly and also the date. (Children could make paint hand- and footprints instead; if so, have additional adult help available and be extra-well organised with equipment and cleaning-up facilities.)

Talkabout

Look how amazing our bodies are. Think of all the things we can do, and how different we all look. We should thank God for making us so wonderful.

TIP
Use good quality, non-allergenic lipstick and check with parents/carers beforehand about possible skin allergies.

BEDROOM PICTURE

Verse

I can lie down and sleep soundly, because you, God, will keep me safe. (Psalm 4:8 paraphrase)

You will need: *Sheets of white A4 card; sheets of coloured A4 card; ball of string; hole punch; marker pen; ruler; craft knife.*
Each child will need: *Sheet of A4 card with verse; a frame; left-over craft bits to decorate; PVA glue and spreader.*

Your preparation

If you have a computer, print the verse on to the centre of the white card. If not, write the verse on the card with the marker pen. Set the hole punch to the A4 setting and punch two holes at the top of the white card. Thread the string through and knot at the back, making a 10 cm loop to hang the picture. On the coloured card mark a border 4 cm wide all around the edge. Using the craft knife on a safe padded surface, cut out the centre to leave a frame.

What to do

Give the frame to the child to decorate using the PVA glue and the left-over craft bits. When they have finished, stick the frame in place around the verse.

Talkabout

If we ask God to watch over us in our prayers, he will. This picture is to remind us that God will keep us safe.

TELEPHONE

Verse

God has answered my prayer. (Psalm 6:9 paraphrase)

You will need: Marker pen; scissors; sheets of A4 card; telephone template (enlarge the template below on a photocopier if necessary).
Each child will need: Telephone (cut from card); safety scissors; glue stick; old catalogues and food magazines.

Your preparation

Make the telephones as large as the A4 card will allow. Cut enough for each child to have one. With the marker pen draw on the buttons and write the verse at the top or bottom of the telephone. You may wish to cut out some toys, food, cars, people etc in advance for the smaller children.

What to do

Let the children cut things from the catalogues and magazines and glue them to the telephone – things that they like, and things to say thank you for.

Talkabout

As the child is cutting and sticking, talk about how God provides all the things we need. Explain how God listens to our prayers. Praying is just talking to God.

All about me

TRUMPET

Verse

Make music to the Lord with trumpets. (Psalm 98:5–6 paraphrase)

You will need: Sheets of A4 card; sticky tape; scissors; marker pen; crêpe paper in various colours.
Each child will need: Trumpet; sticky stars; streamers; sticky tape.

Your preparation

Roll the sheet of A4 card into a cone shape and secure with sticky tape. If desired, trim the wider end with scissors. Write the verse on the trumpet with the marker pen. Cut the crêpe paper into strips to make streamers.

What to do

Let each child decorate the trumpet with the sticky stars. With sticky tape attach the streamers to the inside edge of the trumpet.

Talkabout

God loves us to praise him, with trumpets and other instruments. He also likes us to sing songs to him.

PILLOWCASE

Verse

I can lie down and sleep soundly because you, Lord, will keep me safe. (Psalm 4:8 paraphrase)

You will need: White pillowcases; cardboard for inside of pillowcases; shallow dishes for paint; cardboard stencils; sponges; fabric paint; permanent marker pen (the type used for naming school uniforms); handwashing facilities.
Each child will need: White pillowcase; various colours of fabric paint; sponges; apron.

Your preparation

Firstly, when you buy the fabric paint, make sure it is the right type for the fabric and suitable for use with under-fives. Secondly, check how the paint is fixed to the fabric – one sealed by an iron is best. Use a permanent marker (obtainable from haberdashery departments to mark school uniform) to write the verse on each pillowcase beforehand. Put a sheet of cardboard inside the pillowcase to prevent the paint from going through to the back. Place the paint in shallow dishes for easy access and put a sponge in each. Type out instructions for fixing paint onto fabric and make enough copies for each child to take one home.

What to do

Place the stencils on the fabric and hold down firmly: apply the fabric paint sparingly with the sponge. Follow the instructions on the containers as each make may vary slightly. You can use any design of stencils. Put the pillowcase aside to dry. At the end of the session give parents/carers the pillowcases and paint-fixing instructions.

Talkabout

God never sleeps. He is always looking after us. So don't worry about anything; sleep well.

ME

Verse

God made people to be like him and God blessed them.
(Genesis 1:27,28 paraphrase)

You will need: Sheets of A3 paper or long lengths of lining paper; marker pen; bowl of warm water, face cloths and towel.
Each child will need: A bold body outline; paints; paintbrushes; apron.

Your preparation

On the A3 sheets draw a bold outline of a body with a marker pen, making it as large as possible or draw round the child lying on lining paper on the floor. Write the verse at the top of the paper.

What to do

Allow children to complete the picture with the paints. Encourage them to paint themselves.

Talkabout

God made us because he wanted us to be his friends, and he loves us very much.

LOST SHEEP

Verse

All of us were like sheep that had wandered off.
(Isaiah 53:6)

You will need: Large sheet of paper; marker pen; scissors; sheep template (photocopy the template on page 65); A4 card and Blu-tack; cotton wool; hairspray or spray fixative.
Each child will need: Balls of white cotton wool; chalk in various colours; PVA glue and a glue stick; 1 sheep cut from card; 1 blob of Blu-tack.

Your preparation

Write the verse across the top of the large sheet of paper. With the marker pen draw the outline of a flock of sheep in a fold facing one way. From the card cut out one sheep for each child. One 'lost' sheep should be attached to the paper facing in the opposite direction. During the talkabout session you can move this sheep back into the fold. (This sheep could have cotton wool on both sides so that it can face either way.)

What to do

Children should glue the cotton wool balls onto the sheep. Then, with the chalks, they could colour the wool to make the sheep different colours. Chalk will eventually come off the cotton wool, so if you wish use hairspray or spray fixative to make it permanent.

The 'lost' sheep can be attached and re-attached with a blob of Blu-tack.

Talkabout

God wants us all to follow him. We are like the sheep who is going the wrong way. We are lost without God.

All about me

GIFT BAG

Verse

God loves people who love to give. (2 Corinthians 9:7)

You will need: Paper bags; hole punch; marker pen; biscuits.
Each child will need: 2 plain paper bags; 2 chenille wires; stars or dots stickers; biscuits; napkin.

Your preparation

Make the biscuits in advance using the recipe below. Slip one paper bag inside another to double the thickness. Close the top of the bag and insert it into hole punch, making four holes in the top of the bag for the handles. Write the verse on the bag.

Recipe (quantities given make about 20–22 small biscuits)

120 g (4 oz) butter
60 g (2 oz) caster sugar
180 g (6 oz) self-raising flour

Cream butter and sugar together and fold in flour to make dough. Form mixture into small balls about the size of a walnut and space out (the mixture will spread as it cooks) on 2 baking trays greased or lined with non-stick paper. Press down lightly with a fork. Bake for 15–20 minutes at 180ºC, gas mark 4, until slightly golden. Remove from oven and place on wire rack to cool for a few minutes before easing off the baking trays with a palette knife.

Note: you can use margarine instead of butter, but the flavour will be different and it may be advisable to add a half-teaspoon of vanilla essence to the creamed mixture before folding in the flour. Use either metric or imperial quantities. Do not mix the two.

What to do

The chenille wires will make the handles of the bag. Thread one wire through the holes on one side of the bag, with the ends of the wire on the inside. Scrunch up the ends of the wire to make a kind of knot that won't slip though the hole. Repeat on the other side. Decorate the bag with the stickers. Place the napkin and the biscuits inside the bag.

Talkabout

God loves it when we give presents to each other. It is important to be kind to others. Giving a present is a good way to show how much you love someone.

Idea

You could make the biscuit mixture in advance, keep it in the fridge, and let the children shape their own biscuits. Remember basic health and hygiene rules. While the biscuits are cooking and cooling make and decorate the bags.

HAT

Verse

Obey your parents; wear their rules like you would wear a lovely hat. (Proverbs 1:8–9 paraphrase)

You will need: A4 card in various colours; ruler – at least 30 cm long; sticky tape; scissors; marker pen.
Each child will need: A hat; all your left-over craft bits; PVA glue and spreader.

Your preparation

Place the A4 card in the landscape position (ie sideways) and mark the top centre of the page. Fold the bottom of the page up 2 to 3 cm to make a rim. With the ruler draw a diagonal line from the centre mark to the rim. Cut off the two triangles above the diagonals. Sticky tape two sides together along the diagonals, leaving the rims on the outside. This will form the hat. You could put two contrasting colours of card together to make it lively. Write the verse on one side of the rim. Make sure you have lots of interesting bits and bobs. Include feathers, tissue streamers, pegs, sticky shapes, etc. Wrap chenille wires around pencils to make curly shapes.

What to do

Give each child a hat to decorate with as many craft bits as they can fit on to it. They will have great fun making their creation.

Talkabout

Just as you want to wear your favourite hat or clothes, you should always try to remember what your mum and dad tell you to do.

> **TIP**
> Be sensitive to children with difficult home situations. Always be aware of child protection issues.

STICK FAMILY

Verse

It is truly wonderful when relatives live together in peace. (Psalm 133:1)

You will need: A4 card in various colours; marker pen; scissors; wool in hair colours; templates (enlarge the templates below on a photocopier).
Each child will need: 3–5 flat wooden sticks such as lolly sticks; 3–5 body outlines; clothing items cut from card; wool; crayons; PVA glue and spreader; label.

Your preparation

First cut out body outlines from the card. Next cut out lots of clothes in different colours – jumpers, trousers, skirts, dresses. Each child will need several outfits. Cut wool into short strands for hair. Cut labels to the approximate size of the torso on your body outline. Write the verse on one label for each child.

What to do

Ask how many people are in each child's family and give the right number of bodies and sticks to make each family member. Encourage children to draw on faces and attach hair and clothes to each body. Attach the label to one of the family members and glue each body to a stick.

Talkabout

It's good when families are happy and everyone gets on. Sometimes it does not happen. Sometimes we argue. Try to get on with your family, so that you can all be happy

---

TIP

Be sensitive to children with unhappy home situations during the 'talkabout' session.

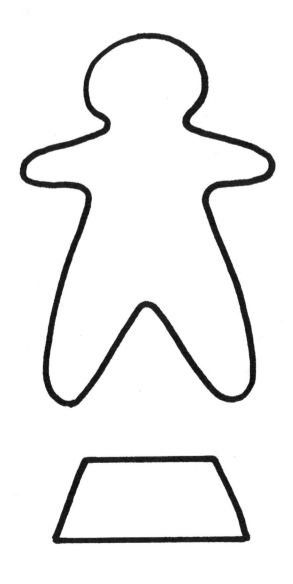

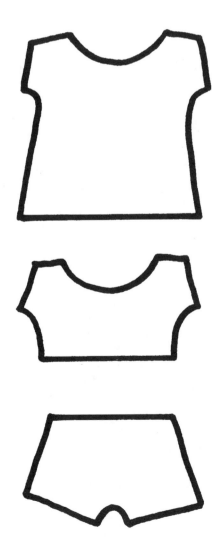

I like food

HUNGRY

Verse

When I was hungry, you gave me something to eat. (Matthew 25:35)

You will need: A4 card for background; selection of magazines; marker pen; scissors.
Each child will need: A4 card for background; safety scissors; glue stick; supermarket free magazines; magazines from aid agencies.

Your preparation

Using the marker pen write the verse at the top of the background card. Cut out lots of different foods for the smaller children, so that they have a choice of things to stick down.

What to do

The older children should choose food from the magazines and cut it out with the safety scissors before gluing it to their background card.

Talkabout

Some people in the world are very poor. Often they are hungry. Jesus wants us to help the poor by sharing our food with them.

Idea

Talk about local or national projects in your area to help those who are poor. Think of ways for your group to do something practical to help. If your church is involved in mission tell the children how you help others.

BREAD

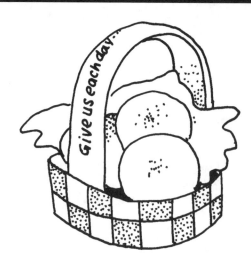

Verse

Give us each day the bread we need. (Luke 11:3 paraphrase)

You will need: Sheets of A4 card and coloured paper; bread rolls; paper napkins; marker pen; scissors.
Each child will need: Basket base; strips of paper; glue stick; paper napkin; bread roll.

Your preparation

To make the basket base start with a 20 cm diameter circle of card. Draw a 10 cm circle on the inside. Cut from the outside edge to the outside of the inner circle, making strips all the way round the circle. Fold these into an upright position. Cut the paper into strips for weaving. Write the verse on one strip for each child – this will be the handle.

What to do

Glue one end of the strip of paper and stick it to the inside of one of the basket uprights. Weave the strip in and out; fix the other end of the strip in the same way. Repeat until child has finished or lost interest. Fold over the uprights into the basket and glue them firmly into position. Attach the handle by putting glue on each end and pressing firmly to the basket. Make sure the verse is showing. When dry place a napkin inside, then the bread.

Talkabout

Jesus taught us how to pray. He told us to ask God for the things that we need.

CAKE

Statement

One for me. One for you.

You will need: Fairy cakes; icing sugar and water; white A4 card; cocktail sticks; marker pen; scissors; paper bags; cup of warm water.
Each child will need: 2 plain fairy cakes; icing; selection of sweets (Jellytots, Juicers); apron; spoon; labels.

Your preparation

Either make the fairy cakes in advance using the recipe below or buy ready-made cakes available in most local supermarkets. Make up the icing just before you want to start decorating the cakes; mix icing according to the instructions on the packet. Make two little labels for each child and write the statement on each label. Write the child's name on the reverse of each statement. Thread cocktail sticks through the labels as if they are sails. Snip off the sharp end of the sticks for safety.

What to do

Cover children up with the aprons and let them spoon on the icing and decorate the cakes with the sweets. Stick a cocktail stick label into each cake to one side. Put the cakes aside until home time.

Talkabout

Talk about sharing today. Encourage the children to keep one cake and give the other one away to someone who does not have a cake.

> **TIP**
> If the icing keeps sticking to the spoons, dip the spoons in warm water to help the spreading.

Basic recipe for 18 fairy cakes:

180 g (6 oz) margarine
150 g (5 oz) sugar
3 large eggs
210 g (7 oz) self-raising flour
Bun cases

Cream margarine and sugar together until white and soft. Sift in self-raising flour and add the eggs. Mix together and place in bun cases. Cook at 190°C, 375°F, gas mark 5 (adjust for fan oven) for 15–20 minutes. Cool on a wire rack.

Note: Use either metric or imperial quantities. Do not mix the two.

CRESS

Verse

I have given you all things, even the green herbs.
(Genesis 9:3 paraphrase)

You will need: Yoghurt pots; paint; cress seeds – about one packet for every five children; sticky labels; roll of cotton wool; marker pen; scissors; A4 card; copies of care instructions; scissors.
Each child will need: Yoghurt pot; 2 card feet; chenille wire cut in half; marker pen; damp cotton wool; label with the verse on; cress seeds.

Your preparation

From card cut feet big enough to stick to the base of the pots. Cut the labels into strips and write the verse on. Make a small hole in each side of the pot to push the arms through. Paint the pots and leave to dry. Cut cotton wool to fit the bottom of the pots. Wet the cotton wool and squeeze out excess water. Have printed reminders to keep the pot in a warm, light place and to keep the cotton wool damp.

What to do

Bend one end of a chenille wire to make a loop for a hand: thread the other end through the hole in the pot and bend over to secure. Repeat on the other side. Stick the feet to the base of the pot, and then draw a face on the side with the marker pen. Attach the verse. Put the damp cotton wool in the bottom of the pot. Let children drop the seeds carefully onto the cotton wool.

Talkabout

All the food that we eat is given to us by God.

I like food

PINEAPPLE

Verse

Taste and see that the Lord is good. (Psalm 34:8 NIV)

You will need: *Yellow and green A4 card; pineapple templates (enlarge the templates below on a photocopier); marker pen; scissors.*
Each child will need: *Two pineapple bodies; pineapple leaves; circles of orange and yellow tissue; glue stick.*

Your preparation

Use the templates to cut the body of the pineapple from yellow card and the leaves from the green. Write the verse on both sides of the leaves.

What to do

Glue the two pineapple bodies together sandwiching the end of the leaves in the top, to make the pineapple shape. Encourage children to scrunch up the tissue to make a ball, which should then be stuck to the pineapple body. Use lots of balls to make the rough texture of the pineapple.

Talkabout

God made lots of good and interesting things for us to eat. We should thank God for his kindness and love.

Idea

Perhaps have a real pineapple to show the children. You could also cut up lots of different fruits, look at all the colours and see how wonderful they are. Taste the fruit and talk about how good it is.

FRUIT BOWL

Verse

Your fruit will ripen in the sunshine.
(Deuteronomy 33:14)

You will need: White A4 card; various colours of A4 card; a marker pen; scissors; fruit templates.
Each child will need: Sheet of white A4 card; fruit bowl; various fruits; glue stick.

Your preparation

Write the verse at the top of each sheet of white card. From coloured card cut out a fruit bowl and various fruits, eg apples, oranges, plums, bananas, pears, grapes, strawberries, lemons.

What to do

Children should first stick the fruit bowl to the white card, then the fruit until the bowl is full.

Talkabout

The whole earth and everything in it belongs to God. God sends the rain and the sun to help our fruit grow. Let's thank him.

Idea

If you wish you could have various fruits cut up for the children to taste.

HONEY POT

Verse

Your words are sweeter than honey, O Lord.
(Psalm 119:103 paraphrase)

You will need: Brown and yellow A4 card; templates for honey pot, bear and bees (enlarge the templates below on a photocopier); marker pen; scissors.
Each child will need: Bear; honey pot; honey bees; yellow tissue paper; 2 wiggly eyes; glue stick; crayons.

Your preparation

Using the templates cut bears from the brown card, and honey pots and bees from the yellow card. Write the verse on the honey pot.

What to do

Stick on the bear's eyes and stick down the honey pot. Use crayons to put the stripes onto the bees and draw a face on the bear. Stick the bees to the pot and bear. Scrunch up tissue paper and stick it down to look like honey coming from the pot.

Talkabout

God has made many promises to us and they are written in the Bible. God's promises are better than the taste of honey or other sweet things.

> **TIP**
> Many children love the taste of honey but it is not safe to give it to children under one year old.

TODOY

This day belongs to God, let's celebrate and be glad today. Psalm118:24

Verse

This day belongs to God, let's celebrate and be glad today. (Psalm 118:24 paraphrase)

You will need: *Various colours of A4 card; templates for tree, duck and sun; scissors; tissue paper; marker pen; blue A4 background card.*
Each child will need: *Tree trunk; tissue paper leaves; flowers, grass, sun, pond and duck cut from card; blue A4 background card; glue stick; crayons.*

Your preparation

Using the card cut out all the bits needed for each picture. Cut leaves from tissue paper. With the marker pen write the verse at the top of the background card.

What to do

Using the glue stick make a collage of a sunny day. With the crayons let children draw themselves and any family and friends they wish to include.

Talkabout

Every day that we have comes from God. We should be happy and thank God for each day.

WINDMILL

Verse

The wind blows wherever it pleases. (John 3:8 paraphrase)

You will need: Thick A4 card; newspaper; windmill sails template; marker pen; sticky tape; scissors; bendy drinking or art straws: thin garden canes.
Each child will need: Windmill sails; PVA glue and spreader; straw on cane; glitter; Blu-tack.

Your preparation

Using the template cut out the sails from the card. Using the straw as a guide, make a hole in the middle of the sails so that they can move freely on the straw. Ensure that the straws fit onto the garden cane. Bend over the top of each straw and push the straw onto the cane until the cane meets the bend. Secure the base of the straw with sticky tape. With the marker pen write the verse around the hole in the sails.

What to do

Spread the PVA glue all round the edges of the windmill. Then add glitter, shake off the excess and catch in the newspaper. Next put the windmill onto the straw. Push a lump of Blu-tack onto the edge of the straw to stop the sails from falling off. Put to one side to dry.

Talkabout

We cannot control the wind, the sea, the sun or anything that God has made. God is in control of all these things.

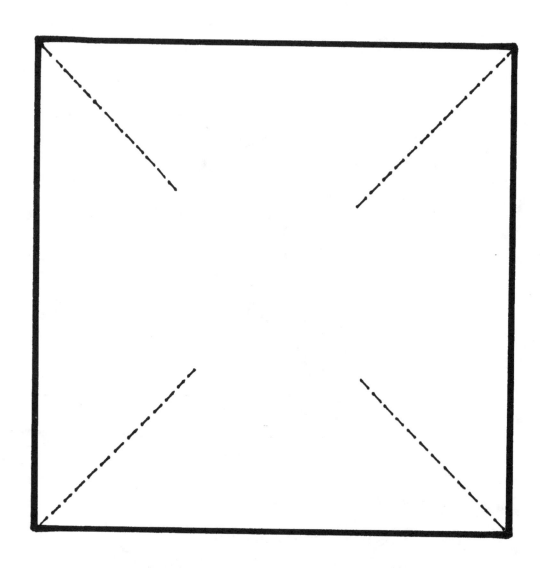

SEASONS

Verse

As long as the earth remains, there will be planting and harvest, cold and heat; summer and winter, day and night. (Genesis 8:22)

You will need: White A4 card; scene circle (below); coloured A4 card; marker pen; scissors/craft knife; ruler.
Each child will need: scene circle; coloured circle; a paper fastener; crayons.

Your preparation

Enlarge the scene circle to approximately 18 cm in diameter, photocopy onto white card and cut out. Then cut coloured card circles 20 cm in diameter. Make a hole in both circles for the fastener to go through. Leaving a border of 1.5 cm on the outside and a small border on the inside edge, cut a quarter out of the coloured circle so that one scene at a time will be visible. (Mark the quarter section first and cut it out carefully.) With the marker pen write the verse around the edge of the coloured circle.

What to do

Children should colour the scenes on the white circle. When they have finished, place the coloured circle over the top and fix with the paper fastener. (Ensure that children take care when handling paper fasteners.)

Talkabout

God will make sure that we have all that we need to grow food and live.

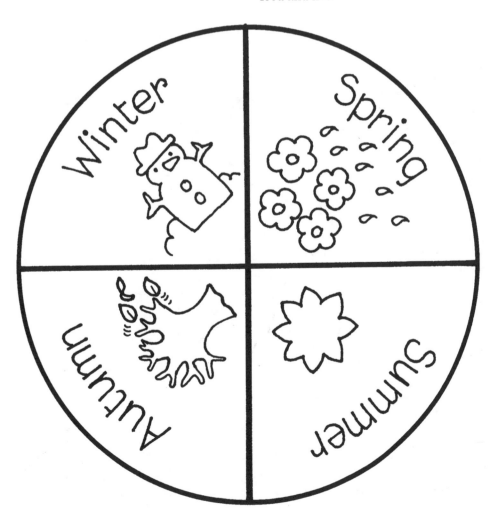

My world

MOON

Verse

When I think about the heavens, the moon you have put in place, I ask why do you care about people? (Psalm 8:3,4 paraphrase)

You will need: Small round balloons; balloon pump; marker pen; scissors; cans of silver spray; newspaper; white card; PVA glue dissolved in water; face cloths, a bowl of warm water and towel.
Each child will need: Small balloon; papier-mâché strips; cut up egg cartons; foil cake holders; small scrunched balls of newspaper; PVA glue dissolved in water; white paint; card with verse on.

Your preparation

Cut the newspaper into small strips to dip into the glue solution for papier-mâché. (See page 10.) Write the verse onto a small square of white card. Blow up the balloons, using a balloon pump.

What to do

Let children dip strips of newspaper into the glue solution and stick on to cover the balloons. While still wet add the odds and ends to make it look like a moon. Use strips of the papier-mâché to secure them and set aside to dry. Paint the moon white and spray on little dashes of silver. Glue the card onto the moon and leave to dry.

Talkabout

Look at the moon; it's amazing; it's so big and beautiful and we are so small. God made our world, the sun and the moon just for us. He made everything because he loves us.

> **TIP**
>
> This activity is better done over two sessions, one to make the moon and one to paint it. Use spray paint outside or in a well-ventilated area. Take care that no one breathes in the fumes.

HOUSE

Verse

Every house is built by someone, but God is the one who built everything. (Hebrews 3:4 paraphrase)

You will need: A large selection of cartons and boxes; A4 paper; poster paint (optional); marker pen; scissors.
Each child will need: Cardboard boxes and cartons; paper windows and doors; paper strip with the verse on; PVA glue and spreader.

Your preparation

If you wish you can paint the cartons in browns, reds, yellows and blues to make them more like a house, but this is not essential. On the paper draw windows with curtains and a door for each child, and cut them out. Write the verse on a strip of paper.

What to do

Show the children all the boxes and with the PVA glue, stick them together to make a house of their own design. Stick on the windows, door and the verse.

Talkabout

The houses that people build are wonderful; some big castles are amazing. Even the biggest and the best house is not as wonderful as the world and all that God has made.

SNAIL

Verse

Everything on earth has its own time and season. (Ecclesiastes 3:1 paraphrase)

You will need: Green A4 card; white A4 card; marker pen; Blu-tack; pencil; template (enlarge the template below on a photocopier).
Each child will need: Snail; cardboard clock face; 2 clock hands and paper fastener; shiny shapes; glue stick.

Your preparation

Use the template to draw and cut out the shape of the snail from green card. The shell should be approximately 19 cm in diameter. Draw a pattern for the shell, and a face on both sides. From the white card cut a circle the same size as the shell for the clock face. Make a hole in the middle using pencil and Blu-tack. Write the numbers on the clock face, and the verse around the centre. Cut the clock hands from spare green card, one long and one short and make a hole in one end of each.

What to do

Decorate the shell with the glue stick and shiny shapes; set aside to dry. Attach the clock hands to the clock face with the fastener, and glue around the back edge of the clock, then attach to the front of the snail. The clock hands should move freely. (Ensure children take care when handling the paper fasteners.)

Talkabout

Sometimes it takes a long time to do things. A snail takes a long time to climb a wall but he never gives up. We need to be as patient as the snail. God can help us to be patient.

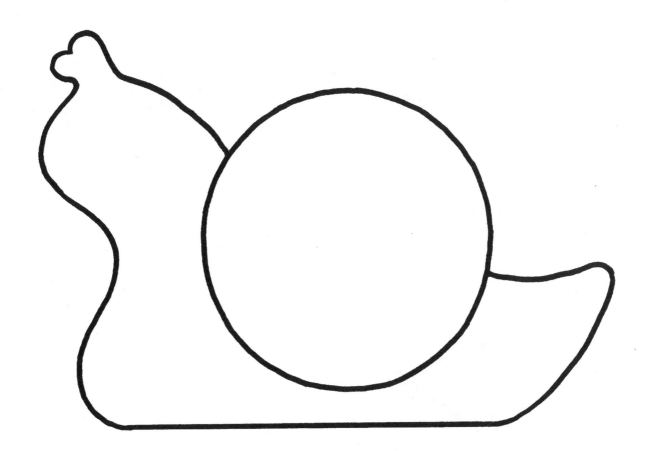

STAR

Verse

I often think of the stars you have put in place.
(Psalm 8:3 paraphrase)

You will need: Silver A4 card; star template (enlarge the template below on a photocopier); newspaper; permanent marker pen; scissors.
Each child will need: 2 stars; thin stick; lametta; PVA glue and spreader; glitter.

Your preparation

Using the template and silver card cut out the stars. With the marker pen write the verse in the middle of one of the stars.

What to do

Put PVA glue onto the back of each star, then add the stick and the lametta to one. Make sure that most of the lametta is showing for a tail. Sandwich the lametta and stick between the two stars. Put dots of PVA glue over the stars and shake on some glitter, catching the excess in newspaper.

Talkabout

When you see the stars in the sky, remember that God made them.

SUN

Verse

From the rising of the sun, till it sets, people may know I am God. No other gods are real. (Isaiah 45:6 paraphrase)

You will need: A4 card in various colours; A4 card in green and blue; thick card for tabs; templates (enlarged on a photocopier if required); newspaper; marker pen; scissors; stapler.
Each child will need: Blue A4 background card with slit; green A4 foreground; tree, cat, swing; sun on a tab; gold glitter; PVA glue and spreader; glue stick.

Your preparation

With the marker pen write the verse at the top of the blue background card. Halfway down the card make an arc-shaped slit for the tab to pass through. Make the tabs by cutting 2 to 3 cm strips of thick card 10 cm long. Cut off the top quarter of the green card shaping it to look like a landscape. Make sure the arc in the blue card cannot be seen. Using templates cut out all the other pieces.

What to do

Encourage children to make up the landscape on the green card, using the glue stick. With the PVA glue and glitter, decorate the sun and attach it to the tab. Lay it all aside to dry. When dry push the tab through the blue card so that the sun is at the front and the tab comes out of the back. With the stapler attach the green landscape to the blue card without trapping the sun. The sun should now 'rise' and 'set' when you move the tab.

Talkabout

God made the sun to give us light and keep us warm. He is a wonderful God.

TREE

Verse

Birds build their nests nearby and sing in the trees. (Psalm 104:12)

You will need: Brown A3 card; green crêpe or tissue paper; marker pen; scissors; templates (enlarge the templates below on a photocopier).
Each child will need: Large bare tree; tissue paper leaves; little twigs, a bird and feathers; glue stick; PVA glue and spreader.

Your preparation

Copy the picture of the tree onto the brown A3 card making it as large as possible. Cut it out and use as your template. Write the verse on the base of the trunk in marker pen. Cut out lots of leaves for each child from the crêpe or tissue paper. Cut out enough birds for each child to have one.

What to do

With the glue stick attach the leaves to the branches of the tree. With the twigs make a little nest using the PVA glue. Glue the bird into the tree and give it some feathers.

Talkabout

God looks after everything he has made. He has even given the trees to the birds to be their home. The birds are so happy they sing.

ROSES

Verse

God's command is to respect your father and mother. (Matthew 15:4 paraphrase)

You will need: Tissue paper in various colours; ribbon; A4 card; marker pen; scissors; hole punch.
Each child will need: Tissue paper circles; chenille wires; ribbon; card with the verse on.

Your preparation

Cut circle shapes from the tissue paper (up to 15 per child). Cut the ribbon into 20 cm lengths. Make little cards and write the verse on; punch a hole in the top to thread the ribbon through.

What to do

Put two or three tissue paper circles on top of each other and then pinch them in the middle. Wrap a chenille wire around the pinched bit to make the rose. The remaining length of chenille wire forms the stem. When you have four or five roses bunch them together, thread the card onto the ribbon and tie the bunch with the ribbon.

Talkabout

God gave you grown-up people to look after you; remember to listen to them and to love them.

> **TIP**
>
> Use paper ribbon from a florist, as it is much cheaper to buy a roll.
>
> (Be sensitive to children with difficult home situations and always be aware of child protection issues.)

Idea

This craft makes an excellent gift for Mother's Day/Mothering Sunday.

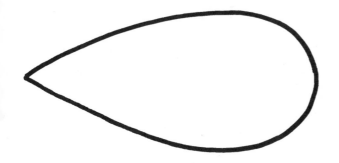

FLOWER

Verse

God gives beauty to everything that grows in the fields. (Matthew 6:30 paraphrase)

You will need: Paper plates; marker pen; scissors; stapler; yellow A4 card.
Each child will need: 2 paper plates; 10–12 large petals; short flat stick; sticky tape; PVA glue and spreader.

Your preparation

Cut out the centres of the paper plates so that you have enough outer rims for each child to have two. Cut petals from the yellow card. Write the verse in marker pen around the rim of half the plates.

What to do

Put glue all round the edge of one of the plate rims and stick petals down. Tape the short flat stick on top of the petals. Cover the inside rim of the second plate with glue and stick down, sandwiching the petals between the two plates. Secure with a couple of staples.

Talkabout

When we go for a walk or we are riding in the car, look at the flowers and trees. See how beautiful they are and remember that God made them beautiful.

Idea

Using face paints, you could paint flowers on the children's faces.

> **TIP**
>
> Use good quality face paints suitable for young, sensitive skin. Always check first with parents/carers in case a child has any skin allergy or sensitivity.

SUMMER AND WINTER

Verse

God, you made summer and winter and gave them to the earth. (Psalm 74:17 paraphrase)

You will need: Sheets of A4 card; weather symbols template; marker pen; scissors; blue cellophane.
Each child will need: A set of weather symbols; PVA glue and spreader; 2 A4 acetates; sheet of blue A4 cellophane.

Your preparation

Enlarge and copy the weather symbols (sun, clouds, rain, rainbow, lightning, snow) on to A4 card and cut them out. If necessary cut cellophane down to A4 size. Write the verse at the top of the sheet of cellophane in marker pen.

What to do

Cover the bottom acetate with PVA glue, making sure there is plenty around the edges. Stick down the cellophane. Glue the weather symbols in any arrangement on top of the cellophane. Place glue all around the edge of the second acetate and stick on top of the symbols; set aside to dry. The PVA will dry clear, so don't worry about how much you use.

Talkabout

God gave us all kinds of weather so that we would have rain and sun to make our food grow.

Idea

This craft can be used as a placemat. It is important to note that it may only be wiped clean with a damp cloth. Do not submerge in water. Alternatively, if placed in a window, the acetate will cling and the picture can catch the sunlight.

SUNGLASSES

Verse

Nothing on earth is more beautiful than the morning sun. (Ecclesiastes 11:7)

You will need: Coloured A4 card; marker pen; scissors; sunglasses template (you can adjust the size of this on a photocopier if necessary); coloured cellophane.
Each child will need: Cut-out sunglasses; 2 circles of coloured cellophane; glitter shapes; glue stick.

Your preparation

Using the template and coloured card cut out the sunglasses. Cut two cellophane circles for each child. Make the circles larger than the inner rim of the glasses and smaller than the outer rim. Write half the verse on the left arm of the glasses and half on the right, with the word 'beautiful' on the bridge of the nose.

What to do

Glue the inside rim of the glasses and stick down the cellophane circles to make the lenses. Decorate the front of the glasses with glitter shapes. Lay aside to dry.

Talkabout

God made the sun; it is so beautiful. Sometimes we need to wear sunglasses because the sun is so bright. God is even more wonderful than the sun; we can't imagine how beautiful he is.

> ### TIP
> Remember to warn the children never to look directly at the sun, even with real sunglasses. It is bad for our eyes.

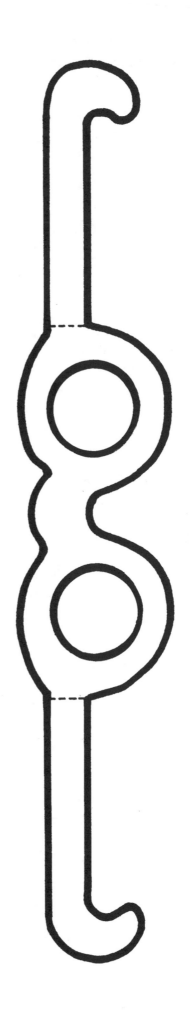

My world

LEAVES

Statement

I like autumn.

You will need: Sheets of A3 paper; lots of leaves; bowl of warm water, cloths and towel; newspaper; marker pen; non-spill paint pots; paint.
Each child will need: Orange and yellow paint; paintbrush; apron; sheet of A3 paper; differently-shaped leaves.

Your preparation

This is a printing activity and needs to be done at a table. Cover the table with newspaper. Write the verse at the top of the sheets of paper. Paint should be in non-spill pots. Have warm water nearby in which to wash hands after this activity.

What to do

Children should paint the back of each leaf, then turn it over and press the painted side down onto the paper. They should continue until they feel they have enough leaves on the page.

Talkabout

God gives us the different seasons – spring, summer, autumn and winter. Each one is different. Which is your favourite?

SNOW

Verse

God covers the ground with snow like a blanket of wool. (Psalm 147:16 paraphrase)

You will need: A collection of twigs; doilies; scissors; dark blue or black A4 card; silver or gold gel pen; newpaper.
Each child will need: Dark A4 background sheet; houses; white chalk; PVA glue and spreader; twigs; cotton wool; white paint; bits of doily; glitter.

Your preparation

Using the dark card cut out the shapes of tall buildings and houses. Write the verse with the gel pen along the top of the dark background sheets. Break up the twigs until they are in small manageable pieces for attaching to the card with PVA glue. These will be used to make a small tree. Cut up the centre of some doilies to make snowflakes.

What to do

Build up a picture of a snow scene at night. First stick down the houses and use the chalk to put a dusting of snow on the roof and lights in the windows. Next build up the tree and stick down. With the cotton wool lay a blanket of snow on the ground. Stick the doily pieces all over the picture as snowflakes. Dot some PVA glue in the sky and add glitter for the stars. With the white paint, add a little snow onto the tree and splash a little on the picture for more snow.

Talkabout

God makes all the weather, including the snow.

IT'S RAINING

Verse

The sky opened and rain poured down. (Genesis 7:12 paraphrase)

You will need: A4 card in various colours; ruler; scissors; hole punch; sticky tape; marker pen.
Each child will need: 8 enlarged copies of the traiangle template below; 1 headband; 2 chenille wires; glue stick.

Your preparation

Cut two lengths of A4 card, approximately 4 cm in width, to make the headband for each child. Enlarge the triangle template below and make 8 copies for each child. After cutting out the triangles, fold in the borders. These will be stuck together to form the umbrella. Cut a curve in the base edge of each triangle.

What to do

Glue the triangle borders together until you have eight, which will form the umbrella. Use a little sticky tape on the inside edges for extra strength. Turn the umbrella upside down and punch four holes on the inner edge, one in every other section. Cut the chenille wires in half and loop through the holes, twisting to secure. Make up the headband by fixing two ends of the band with sticky tape. Measure the child's head to get the right size and fix other end with tape. Cut off any excess. Sticky-tape the chenille wire to the headband to form the hat. Write the verse on the umbrella edges.

Talkabout

God sends the rain to water the plants, and to give us water to drink.

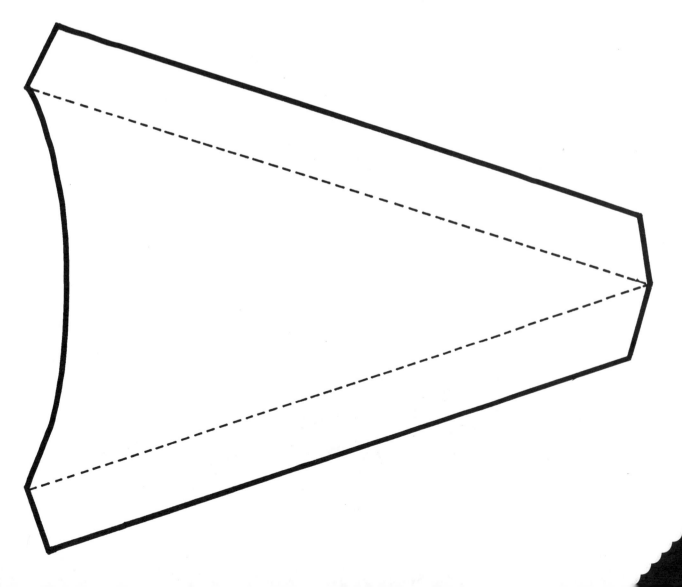

CHRISTMAS WINDOW

Verse

The shepherds hurried off and found Mary and Joseph, and they saw the baby lying on a bed of hay. (Luke 2:16 paraphrase)

You will need: A4 copy of the picture; photocopier acetates (or writing acetates if you have no photocopier); black marker pen; tissue paper, scissors.
Each child will need: An acetate picture; PVA glue and spreader; small pieces of tissue paper.

Your preparation

Access to a photocopier is important for this craft. Enlarge the picture on this page to A4 size. With the marker pen write the verse at the top of the picture. Transfer the pictures onto acetate using the photocopier. If you don't have a photocopier and you have the time you can trace the pictures onto writing acetate. Cut the tissue paper into pieces.

What to do

Let the child cover the picture with the PVA glue and then stick down the pieces of tissue paper. When dry the picture can be placed in a window for the colours to shine through.

Talkabout

Tell the children the Christmas story.

CHRISTMAS STOCKING

Verse

We pray that the God, who gives peace, will be with you. (Romans 15:33 paraphrase)

You will need: Sheets of red A4 card; stocking template; marker pen; scissors; ball of string.
Each child will need: Red stocking; cotton wool; string; sticky stars; Christmas shapes; glue stick; sticky tape.

Your preparation

Make the template as large as possible (enlarge on a photocopier if desired) and cut out as many red stockings as you need. With the marker pen write the verse 5 cm from the top, leaving enough room for the cotton wool. Cut the string into 20 cm lengths.

What to do

Stick the cotton wool to the top of the stocking, and decorate with the stars and shapes. Attach a loop of string to the back of the stocking with sticky tape.

Talkabout

People wish each other a peaceful Christmas. We can have real peace when Jesus is our friend.

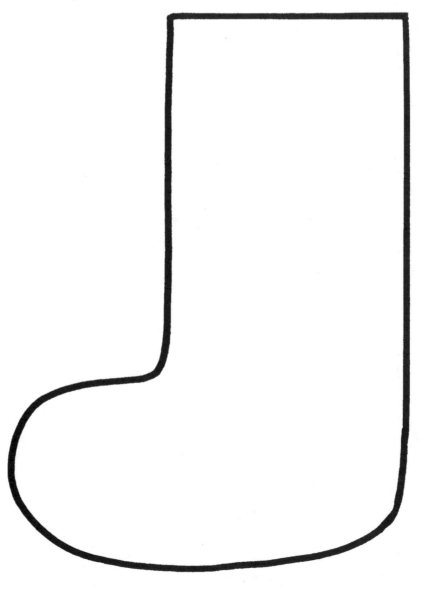

CHRISTMAS CARD

Verse

Praise God in heaven! Peace on earth to everyone who pleases God. (Luke 2:14)

You will need: A4 card in dark blue and white; newspaper; marker pen; scissors; ruler; silver gel pen; angel template; trumpet template (enlarge the templates below on a photocopier).
Each child will need: A4 card folded in half; an angel and trumpet; PVA glue and spreader; silver and gold glitter.

Your preparation

Fold sheets of dark blue card in half to make A5 cards. With the marker pen draw a border 2 cm wide around the front outside edge of the card. Write the verse on the inside left and your Christmas greeting on the inside right using the gel pen. Use the templates to cut out the angels and trumpets from white card.

What to do

Before doing anything else help the child to write inside the card. Stick the angel and trumpet to the card. Put glue onto the angel's wings and shake on the gold glitter. Catch excess glitter in newspaper. Then cover the border with glue and shake over the silver glitter. Again catch excess glitter. Put the card aside to dry.

Talkabout

When the angels sang to the shepherds, they were telling everyone how wonderful God is. God loved us so much he sent Jesus to be our special friend.

CHRISTINGLE

Verse

While you have the light, believe in it, that you might be children of light. (John 12:36 paraphrase)

You will need: White A4 card; red ribbon; aluminium foil; marker pen; hole punch; scissors; oranges; copies of the meaning of the Christingle; knife; cocktail sticks.
Each child will need: Orange with red ribbon around it; candle; cocktail sticks; dried fruit; label with the verse on it.

Your preparation

Make labels from the white card and write the verse on in marker pen. Punch a hole in the top and thread a length of red ribbon through, long enough to go round the middle of the orange. Tie/stick the ribbon round the orange. Make a small crosswise cut in the top of the orange and place a square of foil inside. Remove the sharp tips of the cocktail sticks with scissors. Do not light the candles in your group.

What to do

First push the fruits onto the cocktail sticks. It is traditional to use nuts but these are best avoided owing to serious risk of allergy. Then take the orange and push the candle into the top. Push the cocktail sticks into the sides of the orange above the red ribbon.

Talkabout

This is what the Christingle means. The orange reminds us of the world. The candle reminds us of Jesus who is the light of the world. The cocktail sticks represent the cross on which Jesus died. The ribbon is his blood shed for the world. The fruit is God's gift to us, not only of food to eat but also of being able to live with him forever.

> ## TIP
>
> Candles, cocktail sticks and small children are a delicate mix! Be vigilant and extra safety-conscious. Give out copies of the meaning of the Christingle to help adults explain the craft to their children. Suggest they light the candles on Christmas Day perhaps as a decoration for the table when they eat their Christmas dinner. It may be necessary to cut a small slice from the bottom of the orange to get it to stand firmly, in which case put it on a saucer to prevent juice stains.

VALENTINE CARD

Verse

We must love each other. Love comes from God. (1 John 4:7)

You will need: Sheets of A4 card; sheets of red A4 card; marker pen; scissors; heart template; pencil.
Each child will need: Sheet of A4 card folded in half; heart; glitter shapes; glue stick.

Your preparation

Fold the sheets of white A4 card in half. Write the verse on the inside left of the card. Using the heart template, cut out all the hearts you need from the red card.

What to do

Let the child stick the heart onto the card and decorate using glue and glitter shapes. Help the child to write their name inside along with an appropriate message to their carers, eg 'I love you Mummy...'

Talkabout

God is love. We love each other because God made us to be like him.

HEARTS

Verse

For now there are faith, hope and love. But the greatest is love. (1 Corinthians 13:13 paraphrase)

You will need: Red A4 card; heart template (from page 55) marker pen; scissors; cotton; hole punch; newspaper.
Each child will need: 3 chenille wires; 4 hearts; PVA glue and spreader; glitter.

Your preparation

Use the template to cut out four red hearts for each child. Punch a hole in the top of each and tie on a length of cotton, making a loop in the other end. Vary the lengths. Write the verse on one out of every four hearts.

What to do

Cross over two of the chenille wires and twist to make a cross shape. Then twist one end of the third wire to the middle of the cross and make a hanging loop in the other end. Encourage children to put glue on different places on different hearts. For example, dot the glue on one, spread all over on another, place around the edge, etc. With three- to four-year-olds this helps their co-ordination. (Of course, younger children will just spread the glue around all over the place – that's fine.) Shake the glitter onto the hearts, using newspaper to catch the excess. Attach the hearts by placing the loops of cotton over the hook in the wire and closing up.

Talkabout

We should love each other.

MOTHERING SUNDAY CARD

Verse

Children are a blessing and a gift from God. (Psalm 127:3 paraphrase)

You will need: Green A4 card; red A4 card; tissue paper circles in several colours; marker pen; scissors.
Each child will need: A4 card folded in half; pot shape; tissue paper circles; glue stick.

Your preparation

Fold the green card in half to make A5 cards. Make a template for the pot and cut out the required number from the red card. Write at the top of the card in marker pen, 'Just for you on your special day'. On the inside left, write the verse. On the inside right, write 'with love from'.

What to do

Glue the pot onto the front of the card near the bottom. Scrunch up the tissue paper slightly and stick on top of the pot to look like flowers.

Talkabout

Talk to the children about how God made all of us and how he loves us. God made their mummy; and/or whoever cares for them. We can all thank God for the people who look after us.

> **TIP**
> Children may want to make cards for other people who look after them – do encourage this and assure them that God loves each one of us.

EASTER CARD

Verse

Anyone who belongs to Christ is a new person.
(2 Corinthians 5:17)

You will need: A4 card in various colours; egg and chick templates; marker pen; scissors; pencil.
Each child will need: Chick and egg; A4 card folded in half; sticky shapes; glue stick.

Your preparation

First fold the A4 card in half to make the base card and write the verse along the top in marker pen. Write 'Happy Easter' inside. Next cut out the chick and the egg. Cut the top off the egg with a zigzag line.

What to do

First decorate one side of the egg with the sticky shapes. Next stick the top of the egg onto the head of the chick. Glue around the edges of the egg except for the zigzag edge. Fix the egg onto the card. Push the chick down behind the egg until it is hidden. The egg should look complete but when you pull up the top of the egg the chick should pop out. Help children to write their own message on the inside of the card.

Talkabout

When Jesus is our friend we are made into brand new people. He takes all the bad things away.

FATHER'S DAY CARD

Verse

You know how to give good gifts to your children, but your heavenly Father is even more ready to give good things to those who ask. (Matthew 7:11 paraphrase)

You will need: Blue A4 card; A4 card in various other colours; car, sun and tree templates (enlarge the templates below on a photocopier if desired); marker pen; scissors; pencil.
Each child will need: Sheet of blue A4 card folded in half; tree, sun and car; glue stick; crayons.

Your preparation

Fold the blue card in half to make an A5 card. Write 'Happy Father's Day' on the front of the card at the top. On the inside left write the verse, and on the inside right, write 'with love from'. Cut out a car, tree and sun from coloured card for each child.

What to do

Using the glue stick attach the car, tree and sun to the front of the card. With the crayons draw a road, grass, any kind of background. Help children to write their names on the inside.

Talkabout

Our dads are very special to us. Father's Day is a day to say thank you to your dad for everything he does for you. It is also a day to say thank you to God for giving you your daddy and other people who look after us.

Be sensitive to children's home situations, particularly to those who do not have a father at home. Children can be encouraged to make cards for other people who look after them.

FARM

Verse

Farmers who work hard are the first to eat what grows in their field. (2 Timothy 2:6)

You will need: Blue A4 card; A4 card in various other colours; marker pen; scissors; templates.
Each child will need: Blue background sheet; green and brown fields; tractor, farmer and farm animals; glue stick; crayons.

Your preparation

Write the verse at the top of the blue background card. Using the templates cut out a tractor, farmer and set of farm animals for each child. Also cut out some green and brown fields.

What to do

Give children all the bits they will need to make their farm picture. Let them see clearly what they have and then they can arrange the farm picture as they choose.

Talkabout

God rewards the farmer with good food to eat. God will reward everyone who works hard for him.

ROCKET

Verse

The heavens keep telling the wonders of God.
(Psalm 19:1)

You will need: Black A4 card; silver lametta; rocket template (enlarge the template below on a photocopier); newspaper; scissors; silver gel pen; wooden skewers.
Each child will need: 2 black card rocket shapes; wooden skewer; silver lametta; PVA glue and spreader; gold and silver glitter.

Your preparation

Using the template, cut out the rockets from the black card. Write the verse on half of the rockets with the gel pen. Cut the lametta into approximately 15 cm lengths. Cut the sharp tips off the skewers.

What to do

Take one rocket shape and coat one side with PVA glue. Place the skewer on the rocket 10 cm from the base. Attach several strands of lametta alongside the skewer, leaving about 10 cm showing. Adding more PVA glue to the other rocket shape, stick the two firmly together, ensuring the verse is visible. Dot glue over both sides of the rocket and sprinkle on the glitter. Catch excess glitter in the newspaper.

Talkabout

As the children watch fireworks (maybe on 5 November, New Year's Eve or at a party) tell them to look up into the sky, see the stars and moon, and remember that God made all they can see. God also made them. They may feel small compared to the sky, but God will never forget to take care of them.

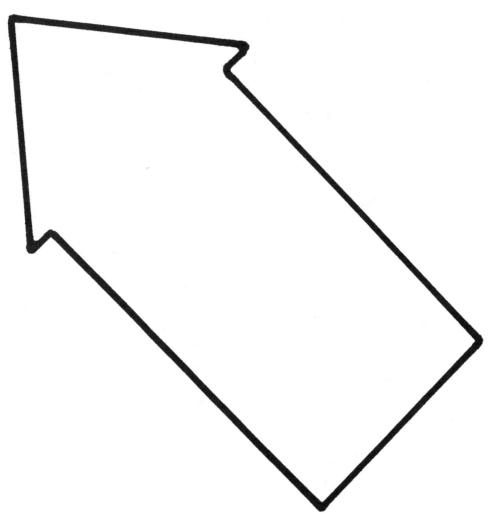

POPPY

Verse

I, God, will remember my promise to you.
(Genesis 9:15 paraphrase)

You will need: Large sheets of red tissue paper; sheets of black A4 card; sheets of white A4 card; marker pen; scissors; sharp pencil and lump of Blu-tack.
Each child will need: 3 x 20 cm circles of red tissue paper; 3 cm circle of black card; 1 long green chenille wire; label; paper clip.

Your preparation

Cut out the red and black circles. Make white card labels, piercing a hole in one end with a pencil point (on a lump of Blu-tack) so that it can be pushed onto the chenille wire and will not slip down. Write the verse on the label with the marker pen.

What to do

Place three circles of tissue paper on top of each other. Pinch them in the middle. Wrap one end of the wire around the pinched area of the poppy, making it secure and leaving enough wire for a stem. This is the back. Turn the poppy over, make sure it has been lightly scrunched and then separate the layers a little. Put glue on one side of the black circle and push firmly into the middle of the poppy. Push the label onto the stem. Fix the paper clip at the top of the poppy stem and use this to attach to child's clothes.

Talkabout

On Remembrance Sunday we remember people who have done something special for us. God will always remember us and the promises he has made to us.

FROG

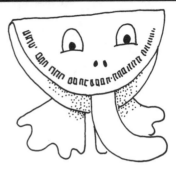

Verse

My heart leaps for joy and I will thank God by singing.
(Psalm 28:7 paraphrase)

You will need: Sheets of green A4 card; sheet of pink A4 paper; marker pen; scissors; sheet of red A4 card.
Each child will need: Green card circle 19 cm in diameter for body; 2 green circles 4 cm in diameter for eyes; pink circle 7 cm in diameter for mouth; long pink paper tongue; 2 red feet; glue stick; crayons.

Your preparation

Cut out bodies, feet, eyes, mouth and tongue. Write the verse on the tongues with marker pen.

What to do

Fold the eyes and body of the frog in half. Stick the mouth and tongue onto the inside of the frog. Stick the feet on the bottom and then glue the folded bottom half of the eyes on the top of the body so that they stand out from the card. With the crayons draw the pupils and decorate the frog. Hold the frog from behind with one hand, open and close your hand; the frog's mouth should spring open and closed.

Talkabout

God likes to hear the frog sing! Think how much more he likes to hear us sing our songs to him.

> **TIP**
> The thicker the card you use for your frog's body, the more the frog will spring.

Idea

Encourage the children to jump and leap to music like frogs. Cut out giant lily pads and play a kind of non-competitive frog musical chairs, using a circle of pads instead of chairs. With the children hopping around the outside, when the music stops they should find a pad to sit on.

The animals and the fish

ANT

Verse

Look at the ant; don't be lazy; be wise and work hard. (Proverbs 6:6 paraphrase)

You will need: A4 card in various colours including white; ant and fruit templates (enlarge the templates below on a photocopier); marker pen; scissors.
Each child will need: Sheet of A4 card; several ants cut from card; leaf, blackberry/raspberry (depending on colour of card), nut and corn silhouettes; glue stick; crayons.

Your preparation

Photocopy the ant template on to white card and cut out enough for each child to have several. From the coloured card cut out silhouettes of various things for the ants to carry. Write the verse at the top of the background card.

What to do

Using the glue stick, attach the ants to the page, then glue into place the items they are carrying. With the crayons draw a background for the ants.

Talkabout

The ant works really hard. To be good at something we need to work hard too.

Idea

Place a small amount of black paint in a shallow tray. Put aprons on the children, and encourage them to finger-paint ants. Draw legs on with a fine felt-tip pen.

ELEPHANT

Verse

The people who are really happy are the ones who hear and obey God's message. (Luke 11:28 paraphrase)

You will need: White A4 card; templates for ears and trunk (photocopy the ear template below twice); marker pen; scissors; craft knife (optional: for cutting eye-holes).
Each child will need: A circle 20 cm in diameter; 2 large ears and a trunk; short smooth stick; paper fasteners; crayons; sticky tape.

Your preparation

For each child, cut out ears, trunk and a circle for the head. Write the verse on the ears with the marker pen. Make matching holes in the head and ears for the fasteners to go through. Cut two eyes in the elephant's face for the child to look through. Where the trunk meets the face fold over 2 to 3 cm of the trunk. Cut a corresponding slit in the circle, to push the trunk through.

What to do

Encourage each child to colour their elephant bits with the crayons first – pink, blue, grey, whatever they fancy. Push the trunk though the slit in the circle and attach at the back with a piece of sticky tape. Attach the ears using the fasteners – the ears should wiggle. Tape the stick to the inside base of the elephant's face. They now have an elephant mask with wiggly ears. (Ensure children are careful when using the paper fasteners.)

Talkabout

We all look for things to make us happy. The Bible says that if we listen to God and obey him we will be happy.

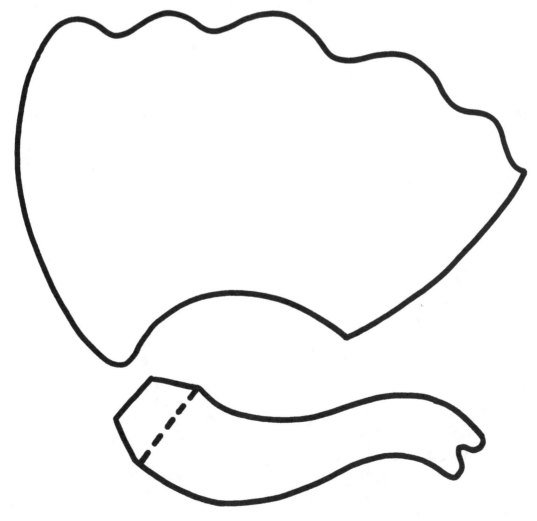

The animals and the fish

PIG

Verse

God made the animals and God saw that they were good. (Genesis 1:25 paraphrase)

You will need: Pink A4 card; pig template; marker pen; scissors; pencil; hole punch; string or ribbon.
Each child will need: Pink pig; glitter shapes; glue stick; curly tail; 2 wiggly eyes (optional).

Your preparation

Make the template as large as possible and cut out the pigs. From the left-over card cut strips for the tail and write the verse on. Wrap the strips around a pencil to make them curl. Draw the faces on the pigs. Punch a hole in the top of the pigs and thread through the string/ribbon, about 20 cm long.

What to do

Using the glue stick, cover the pig with the glitter shapes on both sides. Stick on the tail and give each child the wiggly eyes to stick on if you have them (one on each side).

Talkabout

God was pleased with everything that he made. 'He saw it was good.' Don't forget God made us too.

SHEEP

Each child will need: *2 chenille wires; 4 sheep; a label; 5 lengths of thread; wool in various colours; PVA glue and spreader.*

Your preparation

Using the template cut out sheep and punch a hole in the top of each. Cut the wool into 2–3 cm lengths. Keep the colours separate so that each sheep will be a different colour. Cut the thread into 20 cm lengths. Cut labels from strips of card approximately 15 cm long and punch a hole in one end. Write the verse on with the marker pen. You may wish to make up some hangers for the younger children in advance: taking the two chenille wires, thread the label onto the middle of one and twist them together in the middle; secure with one end of one length of thread by tying a knot. This thread will fix the mobile to the ceiling. Bend the wire into a cross shape and tie a thread to hang down from each point.

What to do

Cover the sheep with PVA glue and attach the wool on both sides, one colour for each sheep. Make the hanger as above and tie on the sheep.

Talkabout

We belong to God and he looks after us as the shepherd looks after the sheep.

Verse

Know the Lord is God; we are his people, his sheep. (Psalm 100:3 paraphrase)

You will need: *4 balls of wool (pink, blue, yellow etc); sheep template (adjust to desired size on photocopier); ball of thread; A4 card; hole punch; marker pen; scissors.*

The animals and the fish

COW

Verse

The cattle on a thousand hills belong to God.
(Psalm 50:10 paraphrase)

You will need: White A4 card; cow template; ball of thread; marker pen; sticky tape; scissors.
Each child will need: Cow (enlarge the template below on a photocopier); a wiggly eye; glue stick; bell; thread; paints and sponge; apron.

Your preparation

Cut the thread into 10 cm lengths. Using template cut out the cows. With the marker pen write the verse in the centre of the body.

What to do

Encourage the child to sponge-paint patches on the cow around the words. Tie the bell around the neck. Stick on the wiggly eye.

Talkabout

Everything in the world belongs to God; he made all the animals.

LION

Verse

Everyone is terrified when a lion roars. (Amos 3:8)

You will need: Brown A4 card; paper plates; scissors; marker pen; stapler; face paints (see Tip); orange tissue paper.
Each child will need: 2 paper plates; strips of orange tissue paper; PVA glue and spreader; crayons; sticky tape; short flat stick; 2 ears.

Your preparation

Cut out the centres of the paper plates so that you are left with the rims. Write the verse across the top of half the rims. Cut the tissue paper into strips. Using the brown card cut out enough ears for each child to have two.

What to do

Encourage children to colour the top plate rim (with the verse on) with crayons. Stick the ears to the top edge of the second plate rim, then stick the edges of the strips of tissue paper around the rim. Most of the tissue paper should be free from the plate to make the mane. Stick the two plates together. Secure with a couple of staples. Tape the short smooth stick to the inside bottom of the mane as a handle. Use the face paints to paint the child's face like a lion.

Talkabout

Some things in life are very scary like the roaring lion. When Jesus is our friend we have someone who can help us not to be afraid.

> **TIP**
> Use good quality face paints suitable for young, sensitive skin. Always check first with parents/carers in case a child has any skin allergy or sensitivity.

SPIDER'S WEB

God made the little spider

Statement

God made the little spider.

You will need: Sheets of coloured A4 card; sheets of black A4 card; circle template 8 cm in diameter; scissors; sticky tape; marker pen; Blu-tack.
Each child will need: Coloured A4 card with a web drawn on it; 2 black circles 8 cm in diameter; 2 long or 4 short coloured chenille wires; 2 wiggly eyes; glitter glue pen; sticky tape; gel pen.

Your preparation

With marker pen write the statement at the top of the coloured A4 card and then draw on the spider's web. Cut out two black card circles for each child. If using long chenille wires cut each one in half. Bind four chenille wires together in the middle, to group the spider's legs. Spread them out a little and bend the ends slightly to make the right shape.

What to do

Using the glitter pen the child should outline the web to create a dew effect. (Younger children will just put it anywhere on the page.) When finished put aside to dry. Taking the two circles, glue the wiggly eyes onto one and with the gel pen draw on a smile. Tape the legs onto the other circle. Then double over a long strip of sticky tape to make it sticky on both sides and place this on top of the legs so that you can stick the top circle down to make the spider. Fix to the web with Blu-tack.

Talkabout

The spider is very small, but it is an amazing creature. Its web is beautiful. You may be small, but with God's help you can do amazing things too.

The animals and the fish

CAMEL

Verse

Let every living creature praise the Lord. (Psalm 150:6)

You will need: Yellow A4 card; A4 card in various other colours; palm tree and camel templates; sand or sandpaper; newspaper; marker pen; scissors.
Each child will need: 3 camels; 3 wiggly eyes; palm trees, orange sun and water; sand or sandpaper; PVA glue and spreader; yellow A4 background card.

Your preparation

Write the verse at the top of the yellow background card with the marker pen. Use the templates to cut out camels and palm trees. Also cut out suns and water. If you are using sandpaper, cut a strip shaped along the top to make a landscape.

What to do

If using sandpaper, glue that to the background sheet first, then all the other elements. If you are using sand, stick down all the other elements and then spread PVA around the elements where you want the sand to be. Make sure the newspaper is under the picture to catch the sand. Sprinkle the sand onto the picture, covering all the glue. Then shake off the excess into the newspaper. Put the picture aside to dry.

Talkabout

God made lots of different animals. Their differences give praise to God. It shows how clever God is and how he has an amazing imagination. God has made us to be like him.

CATERPILLAR

Verse

Don't be surprised when I say that you must be born from above. (John 3:7)

You will need: Various colours of card; hole punch; circle template 6 cm in diameter; marker pen; scissors.
Each child will need: Chenille wire; sticky tape; 7 or 8 differently coloured circles; paper fasteners; crayons; 2 flat smooth sticks.

Your preparation

With the marker pen write the verse on enough circles for each child to have one. Using differently coloured card cut out 7 or 8 circles for each child. Draw the caterpillar's face for very young children (three- to four-year-olds will enjoy having a go themselves). Punch two holes opposite each other on the outside edge of each circle. The fasteners will go through the holes to join the caterpillar together.

What to do

Let children draw the face, and decorate the caterpillar with dots or stripes as they wish. Fasten the sections together with the fasteners including one circle with the verse written on it. Make sure children are careful when using the paper fasteners. Make the antennae with the chenille wires and fix to the back of the head with sticky tape. Then tape one stick on the head and one on the tail. Hold the sticks, move your arms and watch the caterpillar crawl.

Talkabout

With children: Just as the caterpillar changes into a butterfly, Jesus will help us to change as he loves us and we love him.

With adults: There are things in all our lives that we would like to change. Jesus can help. He wants to have a relationship with us. If we turn to him he will show us how to change our lives for the better.

TORTOISE

Verse

The earth is the Lord's and everything in it.
(Psalm 24:1 paraphrase)

You will need: A collection of egg boxes and cardboard tubes; marker pen; scissors; sticky tape; masking tape.
Each child will need: Small egg box; small tube; tissue paper; 2 wiggly eyes; green and brown paint; paint brush; PVA glue and spreader.

Your preparation

Cut a hole in the end of the egg box large enough for the tube to fit through. Put the tube through this hole leaving 8 to 10 cm showing to make a neck. Open the egg box and fix the tube inside with sticky tape, then close the box and tape it shut with masking tape.

What to do

Let children paint the box in green and brown. Make the tissue paper into a ball and push into the tube, leaving some sticking out to make a face. Attach the wiggly eyes with PVA glue. Set aside to dry. When the tortoise is dry, write the verse on the side with the marker pen.

Talkabout

Everything on the earth belongs to God, and that means you, too.

COCOON

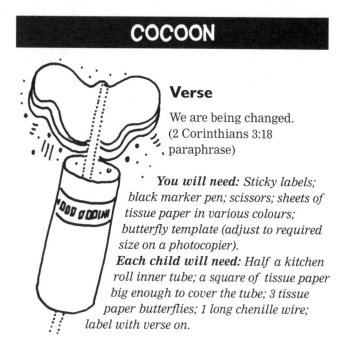

Verse

We are being changed.
(2 Corinthians 3:18 paraphrase)

You will need: Sticky labels; black marker pen; scissors; sheets of tissue paper in various colours; butterfly template (adjust to required size on a photocopier).
Each child will need: Half a kitchen roll inner tube; a square of tissue paper big enough to cover the tube; 3 tissue paper butterflies; 1 long chenille wire; label with verse on.

Your preparation

Cut the labels into strips and write the verse on them. Using the template cut out the butterflies from tissue paper.

What to do

Cover the tube with the tissue paper, tucking the ends in. Place the three tissue butterflies on top of each other and wrap the chenille wire around the middle to make a butterfly on a stick. Stick the label with the verse onto the tissue tube. Push the butterfly into the bottom of the tube. The butterfly can then be pushed out at the top to show it coming from the cocoon.

Talkabout

With children: If we love Jesus then day by day God is changing us into better people, more like him.

With adults: You'll find this verse hanging on the walls of many pre-school nurseries: 'We shall not all sleep, but we shall all be changed' (1 Corinthians 15:51, RSV). Take some time, before your group, to think about the true meaning of that verse and what it means for you in your day-to-day life. Pray for opportunities and be ready to share with others, in an honest and non-threatening way, what it means to be 'changed' through your relationship with Jesus.

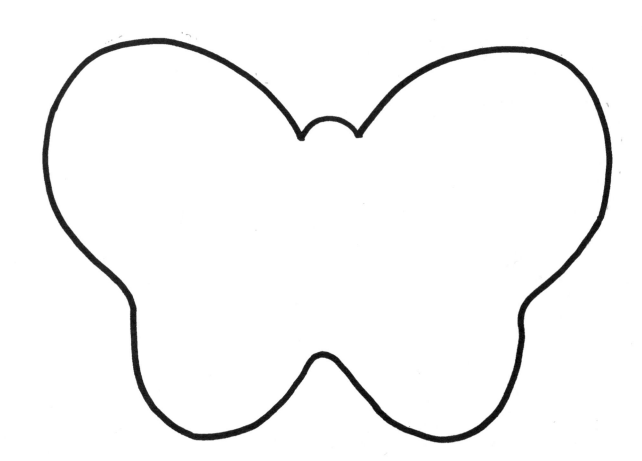

BUTTERFLY

Verse

God makes everything beautiful at the right time.
(Ecclesiastes 3:11 paraphrase)

You will need: Sheets of A4 card; marker pen; scissors; butterfly template (enlarge on a photocopier); chenille wires; shallow trays or saucers; warm water, soap and towel.
Each child will need: Butterfly; poster paints in various colours; 2 x 4 cm lengths of chenille wire; sticky tape; apron.

Your preparation

Fold one sheet of A4 card in half and draw half a butterfly on the sheet, with the centre of the butterfly down the fold. Cut it out and use this as your template to cut as many as you need. Write the verse down the centre of each butterfly. Cut the chenille wires into approximately 4 cm lengths. Use shallow trays for easy access to poster paints.

What to do

First stick the chenille wires onto the butterfly as antennae with sticky tape. Encourage children to finger-paint on one half of the butterfly, using several colours. Fold the butterfly over and press down firmly so that the pattern is transferred to the other side. Open out and allow to dry.

Talkabout

No matter what we think about the way we look, God made us and loves us just the way we are. To him we are as beautiful as the butterfly.

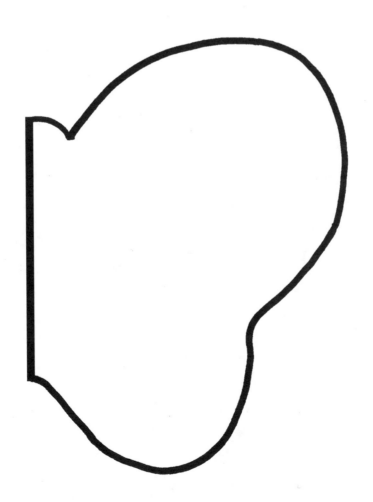

The animals and the fish

GIRAFFE

Verse

God made all kinds of animals, tame and wild.
(Genesis 1:25 paraphrase)

You will need: Sheets of yellow A4 card; marker pen;
scissors; giraffe template; bowl of warm water and towel
for washing hands afterwards.
Each child will need: Bold outline of a giraffe without
legs; thick paint in shallow trays; 2 pegs; 2 wiggly eyes;
apron; glue stick.

Your preparation

On the A4 card draw the bold outline of the giraffe, and
cut it out. Write the verse on the neck of the giraffe.

What to do

Get children to finger-paint the spots on the giraffe. With
the glue stick attach the wiggly eyes and clip on the pegs
for legs.

Talkabout

God made all the animals.

THE SEA

Verse

The sea is God's. He made it. (Psalm 95:5 paraphrase)

You will need: A4 card in various colours; blue A4 background card; sea creature templates; marker pen; scissors; blue and green crêpe paper; sandpaper.
Each child will need: 3–4 sea creatures; strips of crêpe paper; sandpaper or sand in a jar; small shells or sticky shapes; PVA glue and spreader.

Your preparation

Using the templates and coloured card cut out sea creatures: octopus, seahorse, starfish, etc for each child. Cut the crêpe paper into strips and write the verse in marker pen at the top of the background card. If you are using sandpaper cut into 10 cm strips the length of the A4 card.

What to do

Use the PVA glue to fix the sand or sandpaper into position at the bottom of the card. Then stick down the sea creatures and crêpe paper seaweed, along with the shells and sticky shapes.

Talkabout

The sea belongs to God, just like everything else in the world. God made it; he cares for it and controls it.

Idea

Many craft and educational supply shops sell inexpensive stamps of fish and sea creatures. Try making your own stamps using potatoes. After adding the sand to the picture, use a small amount of poster paint in a shallow tray to print the sea creatures.

FISH

Verse

Jesus said, 'I will teach you how to bring in people instead of fish.' (Matthew 4:19 paraphrase)

You will need: A4 card; fish template (enlarge on a photocopier); 30 cm garden canes (sanded until smooth) shiny paper squares or wrapping paper; marker pen; sticky tape; scissors.
Each child will need: Large fish on cane; shiny paper scales; wiggly eye; glue stick.

Your preparation

Cut out the fish from the A4 card, using the template and tape a 30 cm smooth garden cane to the back of each one. Write the verse on the tail with the marker pen. Cut lots of scales (approximately 3 cm x 3 cm) for each fish out of shiny paper.

What to do

Using the glue stick, attach the eye and the scales to the fish.

Talkabout

Jesus wants to be friends with everyone. He wants us to tell other people how much he loves them.

OCTOPUS

Verse

Praise the Lord you great sea creatures. (Psalm 148:7 paraphrase)

You will need: Octopus template; white A4 card; marker pen; blue A4 card; scissors; shallow trays (eg those used for 'takeaway' meals); face cloths, warm water and towel. Each child will need: Sheet of blue A4 card; octopus; various colours of poster paint; glue stick.

Your preparation

Make the octopus template as large as possible, but ensuring it still fits on the white A4 card. Cut out as many as you need. Write the verse at the top of the blue card. Put the poster paints in the shallow trays for ease of use.

What to do

Stick the octopus to the blue background card. Encourage children to put fingerprints along each arm to look like tentacles. Allow to dry. Have water and cloths to hand to clean sticky fingers.

Talkabout

When we look at the amazing creatures in the sea, it gives us a little idea of how amazing God is, to make such wonderful creatures.

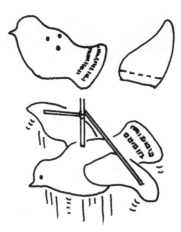

DOVE

Verse

Do your best to live at peace with everyone.
(Romans 12:18)

You will need: Marker pen; scissors; white A4 card; soft elastic; dove body and wing templates (enlarge on a photocopier if desired); hole punch.
Each child will need: 2 dove bodies and 2 wings; 2 x 20 cm lengths of soft elastic; 1 x 30 cm length of soft elastic; silver and gold glitter pens; glue stick; 2 paper fasteners.

Your preparation

Using the templates cut two bodies and two wings for each child. With the marker pen write the verse on the tail. Fold the tab on the inside of each wing. Make a small hole at each end of these tabs. Next, make corresponding holes in the body; they need to line up in order to attach the wings. Make a small hole in each wing tip, and punch a hole in the top of the dove's body; these also need to be in line. Cut the elastic into lengths as detailed above.

What to do

With the glitter pens, outline the wings of the dove and decorate. Fix the wings to each side by pushing the paper fasteners through the holes. (Ensure that children are careful when using paper fasteners.) Next, glue the two bodies together. Attach a 20 cm length of elastic to each wing tip, by threading it through the hole and making a knot. With the 30 cm length do the same for the body. Join the three lengths together with a knot, leaving 10 cm of the longest length free as the handle. The dove should flap its wings as if it were flying.

Talkabout

Try not to argue with others.

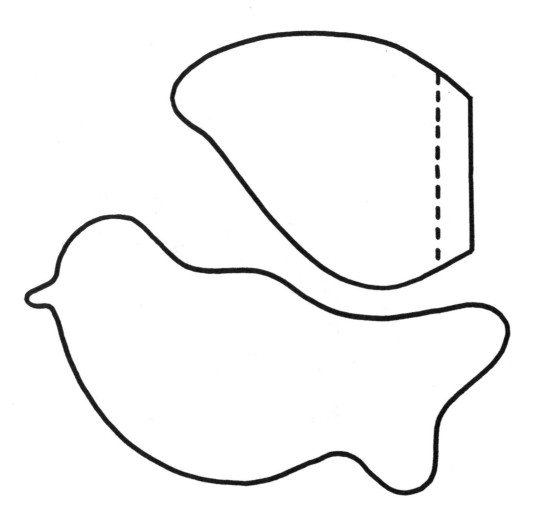

FAN-TAIL DOVE

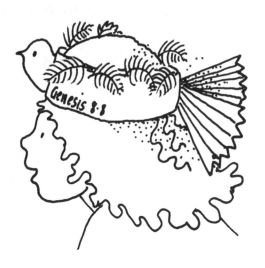

Verse

Noah sent out a dove. (Genesis 8:8 paraphrase)

You will need: Sheets of A4 card in various colours; sheets of white A4 card; marker pen, scissors, stapler and sticky tape.
Each child will need: A circle headband; a dove head; a sheet of A4 paper; white or coloured 'craft' feathers, or stickers to decorate.

Your preparation

Cut each sheet of coloured card into four strips. Staple two of the strips together, end to end, to form a long band. Write the verse along the front of the band. Cut a vertical slit 4 cm long in the front of the band. Cut out the dove heads from the white card and cut a horizontal line in the neck, 2 to 3 cm long.

What to do

Measure the band around the child's head to find the correct size and fix in place with sticky tape. Push the neck of the dove through the slit in the front. Fold over the flaps and secure with sticky tape. Place the A4 paper with the long side uppermost, fold a strip (about 2 cm wide) over and then under until the whole sheet has been folded concertina-style. Fold in half and pinch the bottom, then fix to the back of the headband using sticky tape. Glue the feathers on to decorate the band, or use stickers if you wish.

Talkabout

Noah sent the dove out of the ark to see if the flood waters had gone down. Tell the story to the children.

TIP

If you have an old feather boa (and you don't mind cutting it up!), they make excellent feathers for the dove, as they look like down. Ask at your local charity shop as you can often find one there – especially after Christmas!

The birds

DUCK

Verse

I sing happy songs in the shadow of your wings.
(Psalm 63:7)

You will need: Yellow, orange and white A4 card; templates (enlarge on a photocopier if desired); marker pen; scissors; PVA glue in reserve.
Each child will need: Duck, 2 feet, 1 wing and 1 beak; 4 wiggly eyes; 'craft' feathers (optional); duckling; crayons; paper fastener; glue stick.

Your preparation

Using templates cut out duck, duckling, feet, wing and beak from the appropriate coloured card. With the marker pen write the verse on the tummy of the duck. Make a hole in the end of the wing and a corresponding hole in the duck.

What to do

With the paper fastener, secure the wing in position. (Ensure children take care when handling paper fasteners.) Glue the duckling under the wing and all the other bits in the right position until your duck is complete. Add feathers (if you have them – see Idea) on wings and tummy. With crayons draw some music notes coming from the duckling's beak as if it's singing.

Talkabout

A duckling is safe and happy under its mummy's wing. We are safe and happy when God is looking after us.

Idea

If you have any feathers in the right colours you could stick them to the wing. You may have to use PVA glue if the glue stick does not work.

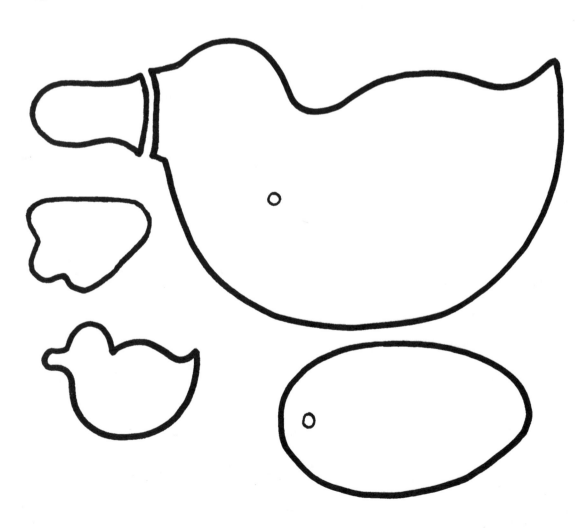

OSTRICH

Verse

An ostrich proudly flaps her wings. (Job 39:13)

You will need: Sheets of beige A4 card; ostrich template; marker pen; scissors.
Each child will need: Sheet of A4 card; ostrich shape; wiggly eye; coloured feathers; glue stick.

Your preparation

Make the ostrich as large as it's possible to fit on an A4 sheet. Cut out ostriches from the beige card. With the marker pen write the verse at the top of the background card.

What to do

Stick the ostrich onto the A4 card. Add the eye and coloured feathers.

Talkabout

The ostrich isn't very good at looking after her eggs, but she can run faster than a good horse. God made the ostrich that way. We can't all be good at the same things. Don't worry if someone is better than you at a particular thing; you will be better at something else.

PENGUIN

Verse

I am God who made everything from the sky above to the earth below. (Isaiah 44:24 paraphrase)

You will need: Black and white A4 card; black marker pen; scissors; penguin templates.
Each child will need: Sheet of blue A4 card; moon; white landscape; black penguin template; 2 wiggly eyes; white tummy; sticky stars; glue stick.

Your preparation

From the white card cut landscapes, new moons and white oval tummies for the penguins. Using the template and the black card cut out all the penguins you need. Write the verse in black marker at the bottom of the white landscape.

What to do

Stick down the landscape onto the blue background card, then position the moon, penguin, tummy, and eyes. Then stick the stars in the sky.

Talkabout

The penguin was made by God, and so were we. God made all the things we see around us. Take a good look around and see how wonderful God is.

OWL

Verse

If we please God, he will make us wise, understanding and happy. (Ecclesiastes 2:26)

You will need: Light and dark brown A4 card; green A4 card; marker pen; owl, branch, and leaf templates (enlarge on a photocopier if desired); scissors.
Each child will need: Owl; 2 wiggly eyes; green A4 background card; leaves and a branch; tissue paper; glue stick.

Your preparation

Using the templates cut out an owl, branch and leaves for each child. Write the verse at the top of the green background card.

What to do

Glue the branch to the background card, then the leaves and the owl. Scrunch up the tissue to make feathers on the owl's tummy. Stick the eyes on the owl.

Talkabout

God knows everything and understands everything. God will help us know what to do.

PELICAN

Verse

On the fifth day God made every kind of bird.
(Genesis 1:21 paraphrase)

You will need: Sheets of A4 card; marker pen; pelican
template; feet template.
Each child will need: Pelican body and feet; feathers;
2 wiggly eyes; clothes peg; PVA glue and spreader.

Your preparation

Photocopy and enlarge the pelican body and feet on to
the sheets of A4 card and cut them out. Write half the
verse in marker pen, on one foot, half on the other.

What to do

First attach the feathers to each side of the pelican, then
the wiggly eyes. Add the feet to the peg by opening it up
and placing the feet in the clip end. Next fold over the
flap at the base of the pelican and using PVA glue, stick
the flap to the peg so that the pelican stands up.

Talkabout

God made all the different kinds of birds.

TIP

When buying pegs for this activity, consider looking
for coloured pegs but make sure that they are
completely flat on the clip end. If you can only find
pegs with an indent you will need to use Blu-tack to
attach the pelican, but this will not work as well.

CROSS

Verse

You are looking for Jesus, who was nailed to a cross. God has raised him to life. (Mark 16:6 paraphrase)

You will need: Thick A4 card in various colours; wool in various colours; marker pen; scissors; hole punch; cross template.
Each child will need: Cross in thick card; sticky shapes, stars, and glitter; PVA glue and spreader; strands of wool.

Your preparation

Cut out crosses from thick card using the template. Use the marker pen to write the first part of the verse across one side of the middle section, and 'God has raised him to life' on the other. Cut the wool into strands approximately 12 cm long. Punch a hole in the centre bottom of the cross.

What to do

Encourage the children to decorate the cross on one side with dark sticky shapes. On the side where the verse has good news, let them decorate with bright colours and glitter. For younger children thread several strands of wool through the hole in the bottom of the cross, and knot them. Older children will be able to thread them through by themselves but will need help with tying a knot.

Talkabout

At Easter we remember that Jesus died on the cross. Everyone was sad, but not for long. Jesus didn't stay dead; God made him alive again. Jesus loves us very much and he wants us to be his friends.

Who is Jesus?

CROWN

Statement

Jesus is King of Kings.

You will need: Sheets of A3 card; black marker pen; scissors; stapler; triangle template, height 6 cm; sticky tape.
Each child will need: Crown; glitter shapes; glue stick.

Your preparation

Fold each A3 sheet of card in half. With the triangle template, draw triangles all along the folded edge and cut them out. With the marker pen write in large letters across the middle of the crown, 'Jesus is King'.

What to do

Leaving the crowns flat, let children decorate one each with the glitter shapes. When they have finished, measure around their heads and staple the crown to the right size. Put a piece of sticky tape over the inside of the staples to prevent them catching in hair.

Talkabout

Jesus is God's son and he is King of everything.

ANNETTE'S STORY

'When living in Helston, in Cornwall, we made these crowns in our Toddler Group. After the session I went into town with my boys, Samuel and Joseph, and both insisted on wearing their crowns. A woman came and asked me where all the crowns had come from. Apparently she had seen about fifteen children wearing them. I explained about our group and why we had made the crowns. Her response was that she had been taught about Jesus as a girl, and had forgotten all about him until that day. She resolved to go back to church and find out more. Simple things often have a profound impact.'

NEWSLETTER

Verse

Shout out the good news of God's salvation from day to day. (1 Chronicles 16:23 paraphrase)

You will need: Sheets of A3 card or sugar paper; articles etc (see below); marker pen; scissors.
Each child will need: Folded sheet of A3 card or sugar paper; news articles, pictures and stories; glue stick.

Your preparation

Ask your team to write the articles, draw pictures or write stories that can be put into a newsletter. They could act as scribes and write down messages and news from the children. Include any future events that you want parents/carers to remember. If possible, articles should be typed. Photocopy enough for each child to have one of everything. With the marker pen write the name of your newsletter at the top of the front page, and the verse at the bottom of the back page. Fold the children's sheets of card in half to A4 size.

What to do

Encourage the children to stick in the articles to make up their own newsletters.

Talkabout

Jesus tell us God's good news, that God loves us and wants us to be his friends.

Idea

If you wish, you could use an A1 sheet of card and turn this into a group activity. Your newsletter could contain information about your group and forthcoming events, and then be placed in a prominent place, or on the notice board. This is a good way of advertising your group and showing others what you do.

THUMB POT

Verse

God is the potter: I am the clay. (Isaiah 64:8 paraphrase)

You will need: Marker pen; scissors; ball of string; A4 card; hole punch; modelling tool.
Each child will need: Small lump of air-hardening clay; label on some string.

Your preparation

Make labels from the card. Punch a hole in one end and write the verse on.

What to do

Give each child a small lump of clay and help to mould it into some kind of pot. When they have finished make a small hole in the side of the pot with your modelling tool and put the pot to one side to dry. Mark the bottom of the pot with the child's name, or decorate the pot with their name. When dry, thread the label onto the string and thread the string through the hole in the pot.

Talkabout

God made us. He is making us into the people he wants us to be.

LIGHT

Verse

Let your light shine so others will see the good you do and praise God. (Matthew 5:16 paraphrase)

You will need: Sticky labels; black marker pen.
Each child will need: Thick, clean glass jar; PVA glue and spreader; tissue paper cut into strips; tea-light candle.

Your preparation

Cut the labels into strips and write the verse on them.

What to do

Cover the glass in PVA glue and stick on bits of tissue paper, until the whole jar is covered. Leave to dry. When dry stick on the label with the verse and pop a tea-light candle inside.

Talkabout

Jesus wants us to live good lives, just like him.

Idea

This could be used as a gift, eg for Mothering Sunday or Christmas.

> **TIP**
> Use a taper to light the candle at the bottom of the jar.

More things to make

NECKLACE

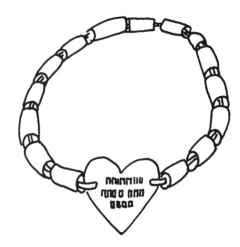

Verse

The right word at the right time is like precious gold set in silver. (Proverbs 25:11)

You will need: Sheets of purple A4 card; scraps of paper; hollow pasta; heart template (from page 55); can of gold spray paint; a length of silver elastic; silver or gold gel pen; scissors; newspaper.
Each child will need: Hollow pasta sprayed gold; 40 cm length of silver elastic; small purple heart.

Your preparation

Put down lots of newspaper and spread the pasta out on it. Spray the pasta gold. Wait for it to dry, turn it over and spray the other side. From the purple card cut out a heart for each child and make two small holes at either side. Write the verse with the gel pen on both sides of the heart. Cut the silver elastic into 40 cm lengths and thread a heart onto the centre of each one.

What to do

Let the children thread the pasta on to the silver elastic from both ends until nearly full. The heart should still be in the centre. Tie the ends of the thread well and push any excess inside the pasta. Write each child's name on a scrap of paper and put the necklace on it and to one side until the end of the session.

Talkabout

We should always think about what we are saying. It is much better to be kind to each other and say nice things.

> ### TIP
> Use spray paint outside or in a well-ventilated area. Take care that no one breathes in the fumes.

CANDLE

Verse

The light keeps shining in the dark, and darkness has never put it out. (John 1:5)

You will need: A4 card; ribbon; marker pen; scissors; hole punch; bowl of warm water, soap, face cloths, towel; tea-light candles; modelling tool.
Each child will need: Apron; lump of clay; beads (non-flammable) or flat glass marbles (used for flower arranging); ribbon with label.

Your preparation

Cut out labels from the A4 card and write the verse on them with the marker pen. Punch a hole in them through which you will thread the ribbon. Cut the ribbon into lengths.

What to do

With the clay help the children to make a pot that will hold the tea-light candle. Push the beads/marbles into the finished pot for decoration. Make a hole in the pot with the modelling tool. When the pot is dry, thread the ribbon with the label through the hole, tie firmly and pop in a tea-light candle.

Idea

This could be used as a Mothering Sunday or Christmas present.

HANDPRINT

Verse

All you nations, clap your hands and shout joyful praises to God. (Psalm 47:1)

You will need: Bag of clay; roll of greaseproof paper; marker pen; A4 card; hole punch; string; scissors.
Each child will need: Lump of clay the size of your fist; modelling tool; sheet of greaseproof paper.

Your preparation

Cut labels from the card and write the verse on them with the marker pen. Punch a hole in one end and cut the string into 8 cm lengths. You will need to work each lump of clay to make it pliable for the children. Cut the greaseproof paper into squares for the clay to sit on.

What to do

The clay should be worked into a fairly round disc about 3 cm thick, and large enough for the child to spread their hand on the top. They should press down very hard, until a handprint is made in the clay. Next, with the modelling tool, an adult should help them to write their initials or name and the date. Let them decorate the edge of the print with the tool.

Talkabout

God loves all the people all over the world. Let's all clap our hands and sing to God, to thank him for his love.

Idea

Make a similar print using plaster of Paris. Mix according to instructions on the packet and use quickly: make just enough for one or two children at a time. Wash up in a bucket or bowl and do not pour waste water down the sink or it will clog the drain!

BUILDING

Verse

There is a time for building. (Ecclesiastes 3:3 paraphrase)

You will need: Lots of junk; A4 card; marker pen; newspaper.
Each child will need: Cartons/boxes; foil and cake cups (junk); PVA glue and spreader; paint in non-spill pots; apron; card with verse on.

Your preparation

Organise a junk collection in advance. Write the verse onto strips of card with the marker pen.

What to do

Cover the table with lots of newspaper to absorb the glue and paint. Encourage the children to build a tower, house, ship, whatever they feel like. Stick the bits together with the PVA glue. Set aside to dry slightly. Once all the children have finished building, call back those who finished first to start painting. This will allow the glue on the last ones built to dry a little.

Talkabout

God made the world and God made us. God made us to be clever and to be able to build things. Look at the amazing things you have built today.

More things to make

HULA SKIRT

Verse

There is a time for laughing and dancing.
(Ecclesiastes 3:4 paraphrase)

You will need: Sheets of A3 card; elastic 0.5 cm wide; scissors; hole punch; marker pen; crêpe paper.
Each child will need: Waistband; strips of crêpe paper 40–50 cm long and 5–6 cm wide; PVA glue and spreader.

Your preparation

With the card in the landscape position, cut into three sections across its width. You need as much length as possible for the waistband. Fold each of these sections in half lengthways. Write the verse on one side of the band. Punch a hole in each end, not too close to the edge. Cut the elastic into 15 cm lengths, loop one end through each hole in the band and tie off. When you measure the child's waist you can tie the other two ends of elastic together to make the right size. Cut the crêpe paper into strips ready for the children to use.

What to do

Put PVA glue all along the inside of the waist band and then stick the different coloured strips on the top and the bottom so that you have two layers of crêpe paper. Place the band around the child and tie the two spare ends of elastic together so that the skirt may be pulled on and off. Don't make it too tight.

Talkabout

God wants us to be happy. He loves to see us laugh and dance.

Idea

Why not put on some lively music and have a dance? You could play a game of musical statues, dancing while the music is on.

CYMBALS

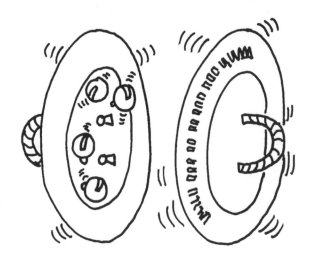

Verse

Praise God with cymbals. (Psalm 150:5)

You will need: Paper plates; pencil; Blu-tack; roll of aluminium foil; marker pen; scissors; cord or ribbon.
Each child will need: 2 paper plates; 4–6 bells; aluminium foil; PVA glue and spreader; sticky tape.

Your preparation

Using the pencil and Blu-tack, make two holes approximately 8 cm apart in the middle of the plate. Cut the cord or ribbon into 12 cm lengths, push one end through each hole in the plate and knot each end to secure. This will form a handle on the back. Write the verse on the handle side of each plate. Cut the foil into small squares approximately 4 cm x 4 cm.

What to do

On the opposite side from the handle, attach an equal number of bells to each plate near the centre. Secure them with two crossing strips of sticky tape. Now cover the whole area of both plates with the silver foil, using the PVA glue.

Talkabout

God loves us to say thank you to him, by singing and making music. Bang your cymbals and sing to God.

BIBLE INDEX

Old Testament

Gen 1:3 God made the light *Lantern* 16

Gen 1:21 God made birds *Pelican* 82

Gen 1:25 God made the animals *Pig* 64

Gen 1:25 God made the animals *Giraffe* 72

Gen 1:27,28 God made people *Me* 31

Gen 7:12 God made the rain *It's raining* 51

Gen 8:8 Noah sent out a dove *Fan-tail dove* 77

Gen 8:22 God made the weather and seasons *Seasons* 41

Gen 9:3 God made green plants *Cress* 35

Gen 9:13 God keeps his promises *Rainbow* 18

Gen 9:14,15 God made the clouds *Clouds* 21

Gen 9:15 God never forgets his promises *Poppy* 61

Deut 33:14 God made fruit to ripen *Fruit bowl* 37

1 Chr 16:23 Shout out the good news of God's salvation *Newsletter* 84

Job 39:13 God made the ostrich *Ostrich* 79

Ps 4:8 I will lie down and sleep in peace *Bedroom picture; Pillowcase* 28,30

Ps 6:9 God listens when we talk to him *Telephone* 29

Ps 8:3,4 When I think about the heavens, the moon you have put in place *Moon* 42

Ps 8:3 God put the stars in place *Star* 44

Ps 19:1 The heavens keep telling the wonders of God *Rocket* 60

Ps 24:1 God made all things *Tortoise* 69

Ps 24:1 The world and its people belong to God *The world* 13

Ps 28:7 My heart leaps for joy *Frog* 61

Ps 32:7 God is our hiding place and keeps us safe *Hiding place* 25

Ps 33:5 The earth is full of the goodness of God *Melon* 20

Ps 34:8 Taste and see that the Lord is good *Pineapple* 36

Ps 47:1 Clap your hands and shout joyful praises to God *Handprint* 87

Ps 50:10 The cattle on the hills belong to God *Cow* 66

Ps 61:3 God is our shelter *Umbrella* 12

Ps 63:7 We are safe in the shelter of God's wings *Duck* 78

Ps 74:17 God made the seasons *Summer and winter* 48

Ps 91:2 God is our fortress and place of safety *Fort* 22

Ps 95:5 God is great and worthy of praise *Tambourine* 15

Ps 96:4 God made the sea *The sea* 73

Ps 98:5–6 Make music to the Lord with trumpets *Trumpet* 30

Ps 100:3 We are his sheep *Sheep* 65

Ps 104:12 Birds build their nests nearby and sing in the trees *Tree* 46

Ps 118:24 This is the day that God has made *Today* 39

Ps 119:103 God's words are sweeter than honey *Honey pot* 38

Ps 127:3 Children are a blessing and a gift from God *Mothering Sunday card* 56

Ps 133:1 It is truly wonderful when relatives live together in peace *Stick family* 33

Ps 139:14 I am wonderfully made *All about me* 28

Ps 145:14 When someone stumbles or falls, God gives a helping hand *Humpty Dumpty* 23

Ps 147:16 God sends the snow *Snow* 50

Ps 148:7 Praise the Lord you great sea creatures *Octopus* 75

Ps 150:5 Praise God with cymbals *Cymbals* 88

Ps 150:6 Let every living creature praise the Lord. *Camel* 68

Prov 1:8–9 Obey your parents *Hat* 32

Prov 6:6 Don't be lazy; be wise and work hard *Ant* 62

Prov 20:24 God decides where we will go and what will happen to us *Feet* 18

Prov 25:11 The right word at the right time *Necklace* 86

Eccl 2:26 God will make us wise *Owl* 81

Eccl 3:1 Everything on earth has its own time and season *Snail* 43

Eccl 3:4 A time for laughing and dancing *Hula skirt* 88

Glitter and Glue

Eccl 3:3 — A time for building *Building* 87

Eccl 3:11 — God makes everything beautiful at the right time *Butterfly* 71

Eccl 11:7 — Nothing is more beautiful than the morning sun *Sunglasses* 49

Isa 40:8 — God's words will never change *Pop-up flower* 15

Isa 44:24 — God made everything *Penguin* 80

Isa 45:6 — From the rising of the sun until it sets *Sun* 45

Isa 53:6 — All of us were like sheep that had wandered off *Lost sheep* 31

Isa 64:8 — God is the potter: I am the clay *Thumb pot* 85

Amos 3:8 — Everyone is terrified when a lion roars *Lion* 67

New Testament

Matt 4:19 — Fishing for people *Fish* 74

Matt 5:16 — Let your light shine *Light* 85

Matt 6:30 — God gives beauty to the fields *Flower* . . .47

Matt 7:11 — Father God gives good things to his children *Father's Day card* 58

Matt 10:30 — God has even counted the hairs on your head *I'm special* 27

Matt 15:4 — God's command is to respect your father and mother *Roses* 47

Matt 25:35 — When I was hungry, you gave me something to eat *Hungry* 34

Mark 10:27 — Nothing is impossible for God *Jigsaw* . . .16

Mark 16:6 — You are looking for Jesus, who was nailed to a cross *Cross* 83

Luke 2:14 — Praise God in heaven! Peace on earth *Christmas card* 54

Luke 2:16 — The shepherds hurried off and found Mary and Joseph *Christmas window* 52

Luke 11:3 — Give us each day the bread we need *Bread* 34

Luke 11:28 — Hear and obey God's message *Elephant* 63

John 1:5 — The light keeps shining in the dark *Candle* 86

John 3:7 — You must be born again *Caterpillar* 69

John 3:8 — The wind blows wherever it pleases *Windmill* 40

John 12:36 — Be children of light *Christingle* 55

Acts 2:19 — God will show his wonders in heaven above *Comet* 14

Rom 12:18 — Do your best to live at peace with everyone *Dove* 76

Rom 15:33 — We pray that the God who gives peace will be with you *Christmas stocking* 53

1 Cor 12:14 — Our bodies have many parts *My body* 26

1 Cor 13:13 — The greatest of these is love *Hearts* 56

2 Cor 3:18 — We are being changed *Cocoon* 70

2 Cor 5:17 — Anyone who belongs to Christ is a new person *Easter card* 57

2 Cor 9:7 — God loves people who love to give *Gift bag* 32

Phil 2:14–15 — Shine like a star *You're a star* 24

2 Tim 2:6 — Farmers who work hard *Farm* 59

Heb 3:4 — God is the builder of everything *House*. . .42

1 John 4:7 — Love comes from God *Valentine card* 55

THEME INDEX

CREATION

Lantern (Day 1) 16
World (Day 2) 13
Pop-up flower (Day 3) 15
Today (Day 3) 39
Comet (Day 4) 14
Moon (Day 4) 42
Space (Day 4) 17
Star (Day 4) 44
Sun (Day 4) 45
Sunglasses (Day 4) 49
Octopus (Day 5) 75
Ostrich (Day 5) 79
Pelican (Day 5) 82
All about me (Day 6) 28
Cow (Day 6) 66
Giraffe (Day 6) 72
Lion (Day 6) 67
Me (Day 6) 31
Pig (Day 6) 64

CHRISTMAS

Camel 68
Card 54
Christingle 55
Star 44
Stocking 53
Window 52

EASTER

Card 57
Cross 83
Crown 84

FLOOD

Clouds 21
Fan-tail dove 77
It's raining 51
Rainbow 18

GIFTS TO MAKE

Candle 86
Easter card 57
Father's Day card 58
Handprint 87
Light 85
Mirror 24
Mothering Sunday card .56
Roses 47
Valentine card 55

HARVEST

Bread 34
Farm 59
Fruit bowl 37

MASKS

Elephant 63
Lion 67
Mask 27

MOBILES

Clouds 21
Hearts 56
Sheep 65

MUSIC

Cymbals 88

Glitter and Glue

Tambourine 15

Trumpet 30

OLD TESTAMENT

Duck 78

Fort 22

Frog 61

Hat 32

Honey pot 38

Rocket 60

Thumb pot 85

STORIES OF JESUS

Ant 62

Butterfly 71

Caterpillar 69

Cocoon 70

Feet 18

Fish 74

Gift bag 32

Hearts 56

House 42

I'm special 27

Jigsaw 16

Lost sheep 31

Newsletter 84

Sheep 65

Stick family 33

Telephone 29

Watering can 19

WEATHER

Clouds 21

Seasons 41

Umbrella 12

Windmill 40

Have you enjoyed this book?

Then take a look at the other
Big Books in the *Tiddlywinks* range.
Why not try them all?

First steps in Bible reading

The *Tiddlywinks* range of Little Books

Tiddlywinks Little Books are designed to be used at home by a parent/carer with an individual child. Linked to the themes covered in the *Tiddlywinks* Big Books, children can discover and learn about the Bible and share their discoveries with you. There are 50 first steps in Bible reading pages in each book, with a story for each day and extra activity pages of fun things to do. Children will love exploring the Bible with child characters Lucy and Liam, Reese, Danny and Krista.
A5, 64pp £2.99 each

You can order these or any other *Tiddlywinks* resources from:
- Your local Christian bookstore
- Scripture Union Mail Order: Telephone 01908 856006
- Online: log on to **www.scriptureunion.org.uk/publishing** to order securely from our online bookshop

" When the Big Books are used in conjunction with the Little Books, children and adults encounter an attractive mixture of stories and activities that will encourage everybody to know and trust in Jesus. "
Diana Turner,
Editor of Playleader Magazine

Tiddlywinks
The flexible resource for pre-school children and carers

Coming soon!
Even more books and an exciting range of Tiddlywinks merchandise...